Now the Soul

Now the Soul

*Free the power of your soul
to reveal secret healing*

Dara Rabel BA(Hons)

Resolute Ventures Inc. (of Alberta, Canada)

Now the Soul

Free the power of your soul to reveal secret healing

©2018 Dara Rabel

All rights reserved. This book or any portion thereof may not be reproduced or used in any manner whatsoever without the express written permission of the author or publisher except for the use of brief quotations in a book review. Any unauthorized use of its contents is strictly prohibited.

Limit of liability/disclaimer of warranty. With respect to all information provided in this book, the author and publisher make no warranties of any kind, express or implied (including warranties of suitability for a particular purpose) and shall not be liable for any loss arising out of use of this information, including without limitation any indirect or consequential damages. The information presented in this book is as a service to our readers of the best intention for improvement.

This book is based on Dara Rabel's personal learning, experiences and deductions. The information contained therein is being shared in this book, not with the intention to portray this as a total basis to replace any previous works on a similar subject matter by other authors but to communicate some thoughts and ideas, which the reader might consider or not, as they see fit.

ISBN-13: 978-0-9952684-1-8
ISBN-10: 099526841X
Printed in the United States of America
First Edition, Paperback, 2018

Graphic design and front cover design ©2018 Dara Rabel

*Dedicated to
my husband Vic
for always believing in me*

Testimonials

I have learned that to be around Dara is to expect a miracle. It's magical to witness a pure soul, like Dara, recognize her gift and share it with those who seek. Her healing practice, teaching and brilliant books are infused with the healing presence of which she surrounds herself. The moment you open the book or go see her, the healing has already begun. She is truly a healer's healer.
Brenda M, Western Canada

Dara has been instrumental in my connecting to my true self. She is astute, skillful and kind. Dara has healed my soul's pain and helped me put my life back into perspective. Thanks to Dara I have been able to find my anchor in life and move forward on a human, as well as, a spiritual level.
Gail V, Western Canada

The special person that happened to come into my life is Dara Rabel. Dara made me aware of the importance to use energy around you to improve your life. Her book *Your Empowering Life Healing Journey* teaches you the tools to achieve to live your optimum life. I highly recommend Dara's healing and teaching sessions. Working with the knowledge she shared with me, I now have the courage to reclaim the appreciation of the essence of my life again.
Anneke W, Western Canada

I go to Dara's workshops to open my mind. Dara is a master at leading us into a meditative state. I feel her book has now done this for me and helped me move on in my life. I am totally happy with all the decisions I have now made in my life, with no regrets, all with Dara's help and leadership. She is an amazing healer for the body and mind. I am pleased and blessed to have her in my life.

Pat S, Western Canada

I always have known and felt that there is more than what we can see and hear, which offers us protection and guidance in our daily lives. Dara facilitated to experience that clearer than I ever had and helped me learn how to develop it more, benefiting my daily life.

Mr. Jan G, Western Canada

I never knew how to learn to relax/stop thinking. Thanks for the guidance/showing me how to see the white light.

'Dan', Eastern Canada

I was first introduced to Dara at her two day workshop....I bought and read Dara's book ahead of time so that I could get to know her a bit. After reading the book I knew there were many layers to Dara and that I would be working on my own development....I was in a place of withdrawing from everything....I knew I had to go and I am glad I did.

Dara had planned an extraordinary workshop. I could tell right away she had taken a lot of time to make everything right. Dara cares for her clients in her own magical way. The attention to detail was unbelievable and it was not long before I was engaged in what Dara had to say. Here was a woman who had spent a great deal of time making sure she had it right before sharing it with others....I was carried away with the content of Dara's workshop. I was made to feel comfortable and able to ask questions....Slowly some energy was restored....I was able to build a strong foundation on the second day that would carry me forward. Dara introduced me to some ideas and concepts that I had not thought about before. By the time I left I knew what I needed to do next....Dara had provided me with direction.

My goal was to be whole again....I began to see Dara for individual consults. I asked Dara to help me make myself whole....Dara accepted the challenge and was more than willing to help....Dara was able to pull things up from my past so that I could revisit them. I needed to learn the importance of each one of these events so that I could rebuild myself. Dara presented challenges and held doors open for me to walk through. It was up to me to do the work....I have had four consults with Dara and I am already well on my way to being whole again. Dara has helped me to figure out who I am and what I need to work on.

Dara is a kind, thoughtful person who gives of her time and energy to help others....Dara is there to help open doors and coach you along the way. I know that my Soul is becoming whole again on my own journey in life. I am happy to have met Dara and the work we have done together. I am looking forward to working with her again. It is an honour to have the help of such a caring person. I would strongly recommend Dara as a soul healing coach to anyone who was willing to do the work.

Peggy T, Western Canada

About the author

Dara Rabel is an author, presenter, an accredited Reiki Master Healer, a certified Feng Shui Practitioner, a Shamanic Healer, Soul Coach and an authority on other wellness modalities. She has spent over thirty years researching the energy within and beyond us, motivating people to attain a more positive 'self' on an emotional, spiritual, physical and mental level to empower their life and reach their optimum. She works with a unique blend of several modalities and greatly elevated vibrational levels of energy, which are attuned to a person's specific needs to bring them healing and release. This unique technique, originated by Dara Rabel, is *Soul Oneness Power©*. Dara's book, *Your Empowering Life Healing Journey* embodies *Soul Oneness Power©*.

Dara sees clients privately for healing and teaching sessions at her practice and provides Feng Shui Healing consultations for both residential and commercial environments. She gives public presentations of her work. Some of the themes offered within a group session or in a presentation are Soul Healing, Heal Yourself and your Life, Better Sleep, Understanding Energy and Attaining *Soul Oneness Power©* to Improve Life.

She lives in Western Canada with her husband and has three grown-up children.

Email: info@SoulLifeHealings.com

Other books by Dara Rabel
Your Empowering Life Healing Journey   November 2016

Acknowledgements

When writing my first book, *Your Empowering Life Healing Journey*, it was a challenge to maintain a delicate balance between guiding the process of receiving pure energy from the highest vibrational levels of energy, yet still allowing the reader to experience it in their unique way. This called for more detailed information about that process and all the ancillary techniques. This is that book.

While compiling the information for this book, the more notes I jotted down, the more information came. This spontaneous creativity generated inspiration upon inspiration, a wealth of knowledge that needed to be expressed.

Special thanks to my son and daughters for your insightful suggestions. I am very proud to have had your encouragement. I appreciated the usual great support from my husband. As an engineer in the oil and gas industry, the term 'energy' had its own meaning for him. Over the many years, he saw tangible, positive results of my work in reading energy and energy healing. Despite his initial skepticism, he did not express this, but simply continued to hear about my work and witness the positive results. Now he is my biggest promoter. Thank you to my sister, Hania, for your work in creating a design and layout for the reader.

I would like to thank my friends and clients, who have received healings. Your validation affirms that healing works and has brought great improvements to your health and lives. Your endorsement of my work has given me encouragement to pursue further potential beyond us.

Dara Rabel BA(Hons)   February 2017

Introduction

This book is intended for those people who seek to explore what is around us and beyond us. Initially, the content presented in this book is as simple as it can feasibly be so that the novice can build on his or her knowledge. This would provide a frame of reference for the reader to be able to comprehend more complex and abstract information. With this foundation in place, a person can then advance their knowledge. Towards the end of this book, the information is quite profound, demanding a certain amount of trust and open-mindedness. A person with no knowledge in this field would be able to read this book and gain the foundational information to begin to understand the truth of their being and their life.

I found that it was more challenging than I had anticipated putting into words my work of healing since what I do is intuitive and instinctive. I do not purposefully think about the process of healing. I just do it. For the reader to understand how healing energy can work, however, I had to disassemble my process to learn what actually happens. Then I had to convert this into words on a page for this book.

My personal research into this huge subject has spanned thirty years. Initially, I read a few books on the topics of spirituality, life after death, life force energy, but it did not begin to answer many of my numerous questions. My quest became focused on healing in the past seventeen years, during the evolution of my own specialized learning. Only now do I feel that many of my questions have been answered, although this does not curtail any future research. With the acceptance that the more related topics I explore, the more areas of learning I will encounter, I recognize that I will be learning for my entire life.

Getting in touch with the spiritual plane, also known as the universe, is not a test whether we can or cannot do this. There is no right or wrong. Each of us approaches this as an individual. Just as we have different personalities, so too we have a unique approach to the way we connect with the spiritual plane and receive its many benefits. If a method already works for you and brings you good results, then it works.

This book is not intended to imply that it is the only source of accurate and thorough information on this topic. I do not profess to be the sole authority on the subject. I do not do anything that other healers, spiritualists or psychics can also do, but it is the unique way I have brought together my abilities that is distinctive. These are totally my own experiences, findings and views. I have witnessed excellent results in my own life and the lives of the people with whom I have connected. I chose to share this information in the hope that it will benefit the reader in some way. My vocation is to help people, hence I have followed my path of healing. My research into the energy beyond us was as a result of my healing work, to find a way to bring healing to people who were going through hardships in their lives on a physical, mental or emotional level. A strong impetus came from seeing a critical increase in the incidents of children enduring cancer. I share the hope that a solution to cancer can be found. Since allopathic medicine has so far not been able to accomplish this, perhaps healing can offer the solution. My work and writing is my contribution to attaining this solution and to propose strategies for improvement in all aspects of people's lives.

I have found that people can undergo a major change on the physical level, the body, during their life, but their soul remains untouched, unaltered and unevolved. The two levels are not separate but are intrinsically linked. For actual progress to be made, the soul has to be reached. All healing can be done at the soul level, but only a fraction can be done at the physical, the brain level. I caution people not to be one of those people with an unevolved soul. Reaching the level where the soul can heal, at the highest vibrational levels, is a daunting task, but if the good results are worth having, they are worth working for. If this book can make people more aware of how to receive the gifts of their soul to reveal secret healing and use this to enjoy more rewarding lives, then my work is done.

Many people already appreciate spirituality, perform their own spiritual work and use this in their day, thereby advancing their life. It is my hope that these people will nonetheless still encounter a benefit from the experiences and suggestions presented in this book.

My own journey of my life thus far has been eventful and intricate, even inspiring. I have learned so much and am now sharing some of this knowledge in this book. It did not do the topic justice to pull out a few random facts to give another person an overall understanding of the soul, thus I was prompted to bring this book into being. It provides the information and the tools to help people attain happiness, health and fulfillment, as it is never too late to achieve this for yourself. It embraces the hope that the personal spiritual evolution and soul healing will happen for many people.

And now, I would like to introduce you to your soul.

Contents

1 The spiritual body   19

2 What is around us   35

3 My background   55

4 The ways to access energy   71

5 The soul   85

6 The soul and energy   109

7 The soul and guidance in life   121

8 Post-traumatic stress disorder (PTSD)   147

9 The first domino   159

10 Reading and healing the soul   169

11 ReBirth of the soul   191

Notes   204

1
The spiritual body

At some point in our life, we ask the question, "Is this all there is?" We ask it as a rhetorical question. If it were to be posed as a literal question, most people would not seek the answer. This could possibly be as a result of not knowing how to look, or even where to look for the answer. We might ask the question and expect someone else to have the answer, without considering that we might have these answers within ourselves.

A wealth of information exists in books and electronically, but how does the seeker feel assured of its authenticity, its truth? They cannot and do not. This is their first misguidance; they looked elsewhere for the answer when they should have looked within themselves. We hold all those answers within ourselves. We need only to trust this and find a way to connect with it, by using the tools we hold within our soul and our spiritual level. We are a spiritual being in a physical body.

We are familiar with our physical body, its internal organs, being surrounded by bones and covered with flesh and blood vessels. In our head is our brain, a physical organ made of white and gray matter, with interconnected pathways presenting specific functions. It is the Central Processing Unit of our body, which acquires information from the surrounding world, stores it and processes it in predetermined, fundamental ways. It controls the major functions of our organs to keep our body alive. Also within us, is the mind, which is quite different from the brain. The mind, being comprised of energy, is elevated from the brain plane to the spiritual realm, where it can see, deduce and learn with limitless ability.

Our mind can send us to experience a seashore when we are standing in our kitchen; our mind can recreate a happy childhood emotion, even though we are forty years old. It is a labyrinth of intricate energy to enable the reconnection to that energy. Everything is energy; we are energy, our home and its contents are energy, even our thoughts and words are energy. Each of these items modulates at its own frequency within the lower vibration band. Our physical body has a finite form but is a large and complex mass of energy and in this way, it overlaps with others' energy and with the energy of objects. If we were able to become less aware of the fixed form of our body, we would be able to ignore our body, thereby unburdening ourselves of its limitations. We would then be capable of freeing ourselves to reach higher spiritual levels, gaining new and amazing experiences with our altered form, our altered feeling and our altered view. During my research, I have spent thirty years freeing my mind to get to the place of profoundly understanding energy so that

I could then work with it.

Certainly, people use their brains, but many people live life exclusively imprisoned within that box in the top of their head. Their life experiences are conducted mainly from the brain. This drastically limits the freedom of their mind, to step outside of that box of the brain. This is the first basic awareness to understanding that there is a great wealth of experiences around and beyond us. We must get out of our head.

I recall at five years old standing in the school playground. I watched a girl playing with a spinning top, the choice of school toy at that time. She had covered the surface of the small wooden top with different colored chalk and, as she hit it with the leather shoelace, it spun in a cohesive maze of colors. I stared at it in awe. I did not have a spinning top, so the girl lent me her top, but I could not make it spin. I returned it to her. As I again watched the colors of the top, my mind deduced that I could leave my body and go over to her to experience through her the fun she was having of successfully spinning the top. This seemed a very logical thought to me. I already had this awareness and was questioning why 'I' was in 'this' body and could not be in 'that' body. I had the inclination but lacked the ability to do this, so I was left only observing this fun.

This thought of going outside my body was enabled by my five-year-old mind, as no restrictions had been placed on this. I did not ask an adult about this, therefore I did not encounter any contradictions that this link could be accomplished.

As a seven-year-old, I began to see colors at night on the ceiling, drifting gently down to me as they formed shapes, small images of a flower, a star and many other images. I was observing energy in a way that a child could understand it. I held out my hand to allow them to land on it, which they did and then they disappeared. Although I thoroughly enjoyed this spectacle, I was, however, in denial of seeing this so that I could be accepted socially by the school children. I did trust my sister to ask if she could see this too. She confirmed she could and this appeased me. It was not until much later in life that she told me she could not see these colors but had said this to reassure me. Since I kept these remarkable events to myself, the belief of things beyond us remained intact and deep within me until I re-discovered it later in life, at a time when I was able to understand its full significance.

Knowing energy as a child helped me to always accept it, never questioning it, although I instinctively did keep it to myself. This has stood me well for my adult life, where I do not question energy in my work of healing. I learned the ability to think outside my earthbound brain-box and have always conducted my thinking in this way. We will become confused if we constantly try to relate these 'other' happenings to our restrictive earthbound consciousness. We need to see it, receive it and accept it within the realms of the 'beyond', to ponder it with the mind of the 'beyond', and not to drag these thoughts back in an attempt to relate them to the restrictive processes of the earthbound brain.

The vulnerability to discerning energy and seeing things very differently as a child is that, whilst being a valuable benefit in the universal realm, it could cause a disconnect with the earthly plane in social situations as one becomes an observer rather than a participant. As children, we view an object intuitively, with an accepting mind. As adults, we have grown up into the flurry of daily life and distanced ourselves from this ability, embedding it deep within ourselves, where it can no longer be retrieved. We begin to function exclusively within the box of the brain, living our repetitive routines. Our perspective is strictly from logic, curtailing any creativity of thought. Our questioning brains become encumbered with these everyday routines, very constricted and incompatible with the limitless freedom of the mind we experienced as a child.

It is feasible that my duality of my physical and spiritual body is as a result of being born a triplet. One of my sisters died at the age of three months. Growing up, I always felt that one part of my essence was with her. We had been connected physically from the very moment of conception, so it was rational that we were also connected on all other levels. I developed an understanding of another plane without realizing that I had done this. This enabled me, in my life, to be open to energy beyond me, to think and 'be' outside of my body. This made connecting with my soul a matter of course. I never questioned it. I just lived it. I have never known anything other than seeing past the physical body.

This does not imply that being born as a triplet is the only way to awaken the spiritual self to access the secrets held by our own soul. Each person will have an innate sense of how this can happen for themselves and attain this by using the tools specifically attuned to them.

As humans, we recognize and work with only that which we can see and touch: our body, our house, our physical reality. We cannot see our spirit or our soul, thus causing us not to manage these directly. This is the source of our limitations in life. It is at the level of the soul, where our work is needed to be done, yet most of us cannot reach this level. This is due to the lack of knowledge to do this, or having no aspiration to do this, or having the knowledge yet being hesitant to apply it. How many of us know what the soul is, where the soul is, what the soul does? How many of us do, in fact, allow the soul to have a significant purpose in our life?

It is a conundrum why we are so unaware of our soul when it is precisely that, which we need in order to receive deep healing of our life. With the dedication to attain the knowledge and the practice to apply the tools to access the spiritual level, a person would be able to open up new layers to themselves and discover that many of their issues in their physical world can be resolved from the spiritual level through the soul. This task is larger than we are, therefore some people turn to their belief in a greater being to open up our spirit. This greater being is known by many names: God, Almighty, Source, All-Knowing, Omnipotence and Deity. Perhaps this is what we are supposed to do and, by being aware of our limitations, we seek the assistance of a compassionate, greater being.

There is a core of pure white light at the center within each of us, which is our essence, linking with our soul. The soul exists on a separate plane of higher vibrational energy within our body. This does not mean that it is higher in elevation into the sky, but that it exists in a parallel plane, which vibrates at a higher frequency than that of our body. Thus our soul at the highest frequency is linked to our essence at a high frequency and also to our body at a low frequency of vibration. The soul is continuously connected to us, at our essence. We just need to learn how to convey from one to the other, from the lower frequency to the higher frequency by utilizing the energy of our essence. The terms of 'soul' and 'essence' are actually not interchangeable, but the overlap of their usage has caused both terms to refer to a soul within our body. Specifically, 'soul' refers to our soul at the highest level of energy and 'essence' at a high level of energy refers to the light within us, which links to our soul.

The soul is like a data bank of our lessons in life, our experiences and our challenges. Traumatic issues, impacting our life, can sometimes cause a piece of the energy of the soul to flee, remain separately, but still be closely linked to that soul. There it remains at the highest vibrational energy level until it can be accepted back within the soul, only after the causal issue has been resolved. The energy piece holds the healing for the trauma and once it has been accepted into the soul, it holds the lesson to be learned by us to advance the soul. This piece of soul energy is very tiny, although totally symbolic of the unresolved issue, however hugely harrowing it might have been. This does not mean that a soul now has a hole in it due to the missing piece since it is only the energy which is missing. The light of the essence within us is affected by this same trauma by being rendered less intense.

For this reason, it is recommended that we invite pure, new, white light through our crown chakra into our body and rejuvenate the essence, keeping it at a higher vibrational energy. A chakra is an energy center within our body and we have seven main ones and four secondary ones. The crown chakra is located at the very top of our head. It has a small symbolic door, which we can visualize to open and close. We would open it to allow pure white light from above us to enter and fill our entire body with white light. This would push along any plugs of energy as the white light drifts through down to our feet, allowing these plugs of energy to exit through the soles of our feet. We would then ensure to close the symbolic door of the crown chakra. This would protect us from unwelcome energy connecting to our energy.

We should strive to resolve the issue caused by the trauma, by reuniting the separated piece of energy with the soul, in an endeavor to complete the soul, piece by piece. Each of us has at least six missing energy pieces. I had worked for two years on retrieving energy pieces for my own soul, by welcoming, receiving and accepting them back into my soul. This process can be conducted by a Shamanic Healer or Energy Healer. I was able to do this for myself. Only until this was concluded and my own soul was complete was I permitted to work, using the methods of soul retrieval, with other people to bring healing into their souls. With an incomplete soul, a healer would not be able to receive the healing solutions or messages from the spiritual realm for others' souls. The completing of our soul is a complex undertaking and will be addressed in a later chapter.

We make decisions daily, drawing various energies towards us. All the energies of all our decisions interconnect, combining to become part of the multifaceted framework of energy within us. We collect and evolve and live as a reflection of these energies. Occasionally, this melee of energies does not serve us well, resulting in drug addiction, alcoholism or marital unfaithfulness, as we strive desperately with numerous futile attempts to find an equilibrium in our life. We then have the daunting task to extract that energy muddle and introduce more positive energy. Most people do not attempt this task, but by refining the energy within us, we have the potential to live life at our optimum. 'Optimum' life does not mean 'perfect', but rather that it is lived within the realm of our capability, while still overcoming the challenges of our life.

We have a toolbox at our disposal. Our brain is a toolbox to tackle life. We resolve life's challenges by dipping into our toolbox to select the best tool to solve the problem. These tools have originated primarily from our parents, our upbringing and society. The effectiveness of our solutions is therefore limited to the type and quality of the tool we use. If we were to have a supply of evolving and state of the art tools to use, our solutions would be much more impactful and produce more satisfactory results. Such a toolbox exists, but we have to reach outside ourselves to access it, as it exists on the spiritual plane and is brought in through the soul.

1 The spiritual body

We understand events with the brain. Now and again, we have a 'gut feeling', which we claim is from an unknown place, so we are unsure whether to heed its information. This is also known as the sixth sense, intuition or ESP (extrasensory perception). People, who are familiar with this intuition, sense this as guiding them protectively or giving them helpful information. This guidance is derived from the spiritual level but bridges the two levels to be perceived on the physical level. It is a brief glimpse into another realm. The total understanding of the message remains in the realm outside of the physical consciousness, but the message can still be received and influence our lives positively on the physical level.

When we get a gut feeling, we should act on it, as it comes from a source beyond us. This intuition is our understanding with the soul, our 'seeing' with the essence. We try, however, to direct this gut feeling to the brain to deliberate and gain more understanding. While rationalizing this feeling, confusion results or, most often, it is discarded by the brain. It is a futile venture to do this. Ideally, the sequence would be to identify the physical body and the spiritual body and use the tools of the spiritual body, solving our issues through our soul. In this way, we would then unite the spiritual with the physical body, so that those benefits can be brought from the spiritual level to the physical body and into our life.

To enable this, a person would need to be able initially to separate the two levels. This is a formidable task for most people. When we solve problems by solely using our brain, the resolution is sometimes unsuccessful and we question the disappointing outcome. We can learn to connect with our spiritual self and receive our solutions to our issues within our soul. When we reconnect with our earthly self, we must use our answer from our soul and not transfer the results to our earthly brain to enact the outcome. A disconnect thus happens when we have the answer in our soul but handle the situation with our brain.

I experienced an example of my brain making assumptions when given a thought to process and drawing a quick conclusion. While helping to sell a relative's house by using energy, I saw an image of a nine-year-old girl, so assumed her parents, the potential buyers, must be in their thirties or forties. This was not so. They were, in fact, the potential buyers and were in their sixties. The nine-year-old girl was their granddaughter, who frequently stayed with them. My brain's assumptions and conclusions shut off any further access to clearer information at the spiritual level. I had been given all the information on the spiritual level and it was taken to my soul to be read, but unfortunately, I allowed my brain to be involved in the processing.

The body is a physical form, but this is not the 'I', as our true being lies inside our soul and connects with our internal essence. Just as our body is covered with clothing, so our essence is covered by our spirit. The spirit holds our personality, our idiosyncrasies. Our soul holds our experiences, our virtues, our love, our learning and our lessons. If we did not have a physical body around our essence, we might all merely be floating globes of light! One would not be able to recognize another. We identify each other from our physical appearance. During our formation in the womb, when the physical body is placed around our essence, life begins and we become unaware of the existence of our soul. The soul brings past life experiences and absorbs the current experiences from the brain, now disconnected from the soul. Some of the pure and positive ideals, therefore, do not carry over from the soul to our brain, and the current experiences are sometimes molded and distorted by negative influences of the physical world. Negative traits in the person's spiritual level and character might be the result. This supports why some people become capable of committing bad deeds. A distinction should be drawn between challenges in life and atrocities. Although we have to face challenges for our soul to evolve, there should be no need for atrocities to exist and to be the victim of this. It is not the soul which conducts an atrocity against another soul, but it is the spirit which causes this to the physical body of another person. An atrocity can never kill the soul.

As a human, earthbound being, we look at a thing one way. As a spiritual being, we look at the same thing in a different and unique way. The view, which operates in the realm where we are present, will take precedence. We need to acquire the competence to go into the realm of the soul and accept a purer view. This would result in a release of the view in our earthbound negative thoughts, something we know we must do, but something we have great difficulty in accomplishing.

Some people have been let down by their physical body. They might have sick internal organs, multiple sclerosis or be infirm and use a walker, so movement is difficult, and they are reduced to spending their limited energy getting through the basic routines of the day. They are focused on basic survival and are not giving the slightest thought to directing energy to the soul to improve their life or existence. In this sad state, they are hindering themselves further. They have innocently initiated the spiralling decline of their health.

Just as we must keep our bodies fed, watered, warm and healthy, so we must do this with our souls. How to nourish the soul and keep it vital will be discussed in a later chapter. Since many people pay no attention to their soul, this results in a disconnect between the physical and the spiritual. Many of us are unable to keep our physical bodies healthy even with the assistance of the medical profession, so it is unlikely that these people have worked on the spiritual self. The physical, the body, is merely a reflection of what is happening within the soul.

Our body is temporary, but we, as human beings, see the body as the entire person and the entire life, since we cannot see the soul. When a person endures the devastating effects of cancer or of chemotherapy and the body begins to degrade, those close to this person see this as the person disappearing. The stricken person's family see only the finite form of the body. The soul, however, is absolutely still intact. There is no degradation of the soul. If the saddened family knew that the soul could be seen and is still pure, still complete, they could take comfort in this fact, but such is the situation that the soul is housed as an essence in a temporary body, now disintegrating. During the final moments of life, the soul reunites with the essence within the body. This is the only time on the physical level that the soul unites with the essence. When the body can no longer sustain itself, the soul, embracing the essence, leaves to travel to the 'other side'. The other side is a parallel realm, where souls continue their existence. The soul's departure signifies death, but only the death of the physical body.

We need to have a fundamental understanding of the two distinct realms: the physical earthly plane, where we presently are and the spiritual plane, where we can regenerate our energy while we are still on the earthly plane. We do not need to die to access and free our soul. We need to discover a way to reach the spiritual realm, where we can heal, unburden our emotional issues, understand our challenges and learn how to deal with them and release them. The spiritual realm is a plane where there is no negative emotion, no loss, no lack of love, no pain, no addiction and no health issues. We need to receive this spiritual knowledge of solutions and healing energy, bringing it to the earthly plane and assimilating it into our life. As a healer, I assist as a conduit to enable this for a person, by using the technique of *Soul Oneness Power©*, represented by images and colors in the book *Your Empowering Life Healing Journey*. Very simplistically, the combination of the image and color energy creates a very high vibration, which is transmitted to our spiritual level and enables our essence to connect with the highest vibrational level of energy to link with the soul. I created this technique in order to fulfill this dire need so that people could do some soul work for themselves and have the hope, then the reality, that their life can be happy.

The process of connection is very simple, yet powerful. Viewing the images and colors will integrate the highest level energy with our energy. White light should then be accepted through the crown chakra. As the white light drifts through the body from the crown chakra, it forms a sphere of brilliant white light at the essence. A lightness will be felt. The brain will switch off and the mind will guide. The sensation of floating might be felt as the physical body is being discarded. Our essence becomes brighter and our energy becomes lighter. We become like the energy of light. Our essence then connects with our soul at this highest level of energy. The soul is open and offers any information we require. When information has been assimilated into our essence, we return simply by opening our eyes.

The alternative process causes fatigue from futile repetition created by our pointless attempts to solve emotional issues in our head. These issues exist in the spiritual realm and cannot be reached from the body or brain of the physical plane. A tool to separate from this binding is to visualize walking up steps, symbolically representing the ascent to a higher level. This visualization technique will serve to allow the mind to separate from the brain. The mind, recognizing it is freed, will seek the more elevated levels above the physical plane. From here, the mind will pursue and allow new healing thoughts to be received. We need to look at these thoughts with our mind, ponder them, but not draw conclusions, as our soul is working on the most appropriate solution.

When we travel to the spiritual realm, we not only leave our physical body, but we also leave behind all the trappings of that body: the despair, the grief, the betrayal, the animosity, the failures and the conflict with others. The spiritual realm is pure, is positive and is simply love. It would be impossible to transport a negative thought into the spiritual realm. Its energy would simply melt away. Love is the purest emotion and also the most elusive. We have known the love of our spouse, children, friends, pets and would be ready to support them and help them. For some people, their encounter with the emotion of love is short-lived and they begin to search again desperately. To know love is the goal for all of us. It is a dichotomy that love is not prevalent on Earth, where we can reach it, but is greatly abundant in the spiritual realm, where we cannot readily reach it.

When we have gathered information in a realm outside of the brain, this information could then risk being interpreted from the consciousness level by the brain. We have to bypass the brain and process spiritual information with the spirit, with the soul. The brain will be inclined to classify information into pre-existing categories and is flexible enough to introduce interpretation into the information it is being given. The soul, on the other hand, understands it verbatim and there is no need for interpretation. In this way, it is truth.

The following is an analogy to illustrate how well or inadequately spiritual energy can be accessed. You are in a room with only a window into an adjacent room, which is a sunroom. The sunroom is empty except for a basin made of stones in the center. You see a jet of water come up from the basin, high into the air. The fountain spray rises and drops into the basin. The water looks cool and refreshing. You feel an urge to get into that room and put your hand into the water spray. Any attempt to feel the spray from the room you are in would be futile. Calmly, you concentrate your focus on the need to get into that room. You look for any door in the wall and notice a faint square outline. You press it and a door opens. You enter the room and approach the fountain, putting your hand into the spray. The room you were first in represents the present physical existence. The adjacent room with the fountain is your spiritual existence, with the water representing your spiritual energy. If we do not reach our spiritual energy, we cannot enjoy its benefits. We must find a way to reach it.

When we meditate and leave our physical body and travel to another realm, and are later asked to describe that experience, words such as 'wonderful', 'beautiful', 'filled with love' would be used. If we were to describe a day in our week, it would most likely include phrases such as "the driver cut me off", "the store clerk overcharged me" or "I was late for an appointment". These are negative events, creating negative emotions. When we leave the physical realm, we encounter only positive, love, joy, enabling the regeneration of our spirit. There is, therefore, a divergence between the soul knowing it needs love to grow and the consciousness unintentionally blocking that from happening, primarily as a result of our day-to-day trials, the negative emotions, the negative words and the negative reciprocal actions. We have five human senses. When we get in touch with our spirituality, we receive a new spiritual insight. We can travel to that plane where we are no longer limited by our earthly senses and no longer limited by our physical body.

At Christmastime, there is wonderful happiness around. We sense this and pick this up, making us happier too. This indicates that when the positive emotions are prevalent, people are quite capable of sensing energy, discerning whether it is positive or not and bringing the positive energy into their being. If only this end of the year feeling could flourish for all of us all year long.

2
What is around us

To understand what is around us, we must first understand what is within us to be used as a tool, to then discover what is around us. This might appear as a conundrum. The two are intrinsically linked, but the step of knowing our inner self must be completed first.

If we become aware of our self, of our body, we can start to feel separate from our self, yet still be in our body. While walking, allow yourself to be mindful of yourself walking, similar to observing another person but you are observing yourself. Your mind, as you, not your brain, is controlling this perception. Rather than being subjected to the very rudimentary logic of your brain, you are circumventing this and enabling the mind to take control. Thus begins your learning of the ability to get into the mind, which is the key to seeing what is beyond you. This parallels moving from the conscious state into the subconscious state, while still being in the conscious state. This can very easily be accomplished in the sleep state but is a challenging feat in the wakeful mode.

During the experience of falling asleep, an opportunity is presented to separate from our self. As we drift off to sleep at night, our brain transitions through various brain wave frequencies; from the cognitive and processing gamma and beta waves, to the relaxation and sleep of the alpha and theta waves and to the deep sleep of the delta waves.

During the transition between wakefulness and sleep, which lasts only a few minutes, we are in limbo between two states of consciousness. We experience some aspects of wakefulness mixed with some elements of sleep. This state between wakefulness and sleep has been given the term hypnagogia. In this stage, there is the presence of both alpha brain waves, which are the dominant brain waves for the relaxed conscious state, and theta waves, which are associated with restorative sleep. Usually, these brain waves happen separately but they are combined in the hypnagogic state.

This transition into alpha waves and further into theta waves is the entrance to the subconscious mind. It is the first opportunity to access a free mind, although it is very difficult to remain within this stage for very long. The combined brain waves in this stage can generate lucid dream-like visions, where we are conscious enough to be aware that this is happening.

In deep sleep, we reach the delta waves, the entry to our higher self, our mind in its authentic state within the universe. Experiences of the theta and delta waves cannot be seen or heard from the conscious, wakeful plane. It is challenging to recall any experiences at all since it is a struggle to return with them to the conscious mind. Generally, what is created in the deep subconscious mind, stays in the subconscious mind. Our connection to our higher self will give us meaningful clarity on problems we are facing in our life, but the challenge is to return with this enlightenment and to have the consciousness receive it. Only then can we be aware of the constructive information we have acquired, which we can implement into our life to bring positive results. It is quite possible to achieve this, although it demands years of practice and diligence. A more feasible way is to enact the soul, which is much more direct and very effective.

In the deep sleep state, when the higher self is unlocked, I am able to see clearly people and places existing beyond me. I recognize that this is not a dream. From years of using this process frequently, my mind is now able to go beyond my physical being while I am awake to see images of people and places, which relate to the person, with whom I am working in a healing capacity. Each person will see different images beyond them, which will be the images to help them in obtaining answers to the issues in their life. For my work in healing, I have needed to enhance how I see informative images, not only for myself but primarily for the people wanting to be healed.

As a very young child, I intuitively understood that my mind was not locked within a part of my physical body and that it was the tool to enable my spirit to roam around freely. I perceived this to be the norm. No boundary had had the opportunity to constrain my mind, so that block had never been created. As we grow up in reality, we are surrounded by boundaries: of our mind, of our consciousness and of our physical ability. We can, however, push ourselves through any boundary, much the same as a training Olympic athlete finds that extra strength they believed they did not have, precipitating an improvement in their performance. In this way, we are able to step outside into a realm with no boundaries, where it is limitless.

We might pose the question why we would need to know what is beyond us. Can we not be content to wake up in the morning, eat breakfast, go about our daily routine of going to work or taking children to school, arrive back home to pursue evening activities? We could be content with this, but what of the evolution of our soul? Do these daily routines advance or challenge our soul? Even within these constricted routines, challenges could arise: a child could become sick; a person could lose their job and have no income to retain a home; the abuse in a relationship could escalate. When we find ourselves caught in such situations, most of us persist in desperately searching for solutions within our limited realm of reference, within the brain. Frustrated, when the situation is not eradicated or does not improve, we undergo stress and our life begins to deteriorate. Spiralling down, we are unable to catch ourselves. The brain provides the ready, basic solution; we are depressed. Our physical health is now impacted and we spiral down even more. One adverse situation is given the power to convert a seamless daily life into a life of depression, physical ailment or relationship stress. How could this be prevented from happening? By simply not allowing it to happen in the first instance, or at least by not allowing an existing harmful situation from intensifying further. Challenges will be brought into our lives as opportunities for the soul to deal with them and thereby evolve. We can meet these challenges and solve them with different tools other than the brain, preventing the negative spiralling from ever gaining traction.

These agonies of our life must be accessed only from the spiritual level, only from the soul. In the futile attempt to continue to access them from the physical level and with no apparent resolution, this will then reflect in the condition of the physical level, the body, usually with an illness. In this way, the degeneration of the physical causes the further de-escalation of the soundness of the emotional and mental levels. The solution lies in the spiritual level.

We heal ourselves by focusing on what we believe is in need of healing. In our consciousness, we cling to an intrinsic sense of beliefs we have grown up with, which actually do not serve us totally, with the notion that it is an integral part of our psyche. These sentiments, existing as energy within us, can sometimes cause us restlessness, un-fulfillment or a feeling of being lost. Some of these emotions have transformed into fear, blocking us from being confident with other people, or from taking on a demanding job or from going on an adventure. We begin to reflect the fear of failure. Clearing this stuck energy from within us is not the entire solution; we have to learn to identify these sentiments, find their source and release them. Learning the process of release can be very difficult, as we might believe we are surrendering a deep part of ourselves. Release is the key. Subconsciously, a person might want to cling to an illness as security, not fully realizing that it is an illness to which they are clinging. This distortion happens due to the disconnect between the perception in the subconscious and the consciousness. It is an involved and emotionally painful process to identify those feelings, which do not serve us well. We should locate them, within our present, or in our childhood, or in our past lives, and bring them into our present so that we can release them. We will be healthier on all levels as a result.

Once a new perception is attained, we have to work on keeping this new attitude. Like a piece of memory foam, which will spring back to its original shape after being altered, so our brain will attempt to return to the comfortable, the familiar and the entrenched.

The first step to the changed attitude is to learn what is around us. We all want the same thing from life: to be happy, to be healthy and to find love. We must ask ourselves if we have been successful in bringing this into our life. If not, then where is the happiness, the health or the love? They are elusive to us if we are trying to find them in the remnants of a broken family, in the heartbreak of an argumentative relationship or in the ashes of a vindictive world. The happiness and love lie beyond and can be brought into our reality through our soul, and accepted by the soul so that it overflows into our physical reality, then bringing us health. Only in this way and only with the full and true acknowledgment within the soul will we have happiness.

There is no need, however, to search for the tools to achieve this, as all the necessary tools are within each one of us. The principal tool is the soul. Your first step is to have a list of the elements you wish to bring into your life, those you wish to change or those you wish to remove from your life. You must be very precise in your wording; merely requesting happiness is insufficient. You must ascertain exactly what the happiness constitutes and state it. If happiness means more money, then elaborate further and state what the money should bring, for example, the opportunity to pay for a university education for your child.

If these positive changes have not already happened, then we must ask ourselves whether we have even been endeavoring to bring these elements into our life. Perhaps we have been merely hoping the improvement would happen. Hoping might help somewhat, but probably will not achieve the positive end results.

If you could see the happiness, the love nine feet away from you and it could be yours if you would walk there, take it and bring it into your life, would you walk there? Most likely everybody would walk there. This is exactly the case, with the exception that we cannot actually see with our physical eyes the happiness and love nine feet away. The step by step process will be described in a later chapter.

Positive emotions are constantly with us, but they are blanketed with sadness, depression and anger. If those emotions, which do not serve us, were removed, the pure emotions would have the opportunity to come to the surface, where they could have a positive effect on us and on our life. The task is to unlock these positive emotions by eradicating the negative emotions which are obscuring them.

We carry emotional baggage from our whole life and this becomes part of our fibre. We play the same demeaning tapes on our mental level. The energy of those disparaging tapes then resides within us, influencing our thoughts and our beliefs for our entire life. This can be improved by dumping the tapes. The soul is willing, but the brain is reluctant, leaving us caught in a constant see-saw of emotions. We find we repeat the same things in the now while waiting for the good things to happen in the future. Such is the snare of hope.

It is not a matter of where you have been; it is a matter of where you are now. If you were to detach from your life in order to observe, you could see the monotony of your day to day living and therefore see the mundane things to which you have attributed importance. Become an observer as well as a participant. If you are primarily a participant, you cannot have the opportunity to be an observer. When you examine some elements in your life and find that you are unhappy with your observations, this will prompt change.

Each of us deserves to live our best life. A motto that guides us to achieve this is the axiom: 'Live with no regrets'. Take a moment to place this gauge over your own life events. Changes cannot be obviously made to past events, although your perception of them can certainly be adjusted. Modifications can be made to all events, going forward. You need to take the next step in deciding how to improve your life. We all have areas of our personal traits or activities in our life, which we wish to improve. We all have failings; this is what makes us human. The human spirit is powerful, impressive and extraordinary. We can consider this our claim. Each one of us carries this vast potential within us.

As an analogy of why change is paramount, imagine a vase of fresh flowers. Everything supports that they will bloom, look healthy and vibrant, but this is not the case. They appear to wilt and dry up. Why is this? Because there is no water in the vase. Putting the water into the vase will nourish the flowers and make them thrive. This is equivalent to receiving positive energy to nurture our body. Just as the flowers will thrive in water, so will our body and life flourish, revitalized with pure, new energy.

The words are easier to accept than the deed to be done. Most people will have an issue in seeking new energy from the soul, as they have the block of fear. This fear emotion has a web, which spreads and subverts their positive outlook, extending into their self-esteem and into their trust of themselves and others. The fear creates a very effective block to their essence. Being unable to access their essence allows the web to become stronger and support more negative emotions to develop, reinforcing the block even more. So continues the cycle, if it is not broken. The fear then morphs into hatred and then into violence. Negative issues will keep replicating and will continue to degenerate their life and then translate into the degeneration of their body, resulting in serious illness, even cancer.

As a primary step, begin to understand self-love. This might sound like a cliché, but it is a valuable concept. Everybody has love within themselves. Direct your love to yourself and feel the warmth. It will emanate from you and touch others, forming a delicate fabric of love, encompassing many people. Their lives are improved from your radiating love and you have taken a step to experience self-love. Realizing you have love, can give love and are loved, enables you to release fear. These two emotions cannot co-exist. This is the reason why love is so important in the world, as it will drive out the fear, hatred and violence.

We are not living merely to receive acclamation from those around us or to amass great financial wealth. Soul advancement is the necessary objective. We have chosen challenges for our life and now need to go through them, by living our life on this Earth. This will be discussed more in-depth in a later chapter.

We have a body, spirit and a soul. We are familiar with our body. Some believe the body often lets them down with its sickness, its corpulence and its lack of energy. Our brain has activities it wishes to accomplish, but our body curtails this, as it is not energetically capable. Thus we feel disappointment.

We are less familiar with our spirit. Our spirit is temporary, associated with our present body and personality. The spirit is like a coat of energy around our essence. It is the energy that allows us to travel outside of our body, to link with our soul. It also affords us protection from unwelcome energy and receives the energy for the gut feeling. Sometimes we might feel this as goose-bumps on our skin. The spirit is thus the bridge between the physical body and the soul.

Most people are very unfamiliar with our soul, what it is, where it is, what it does. The soul and spirit are linked. It is at the level of the soul where our potential of power over our life exists and where anything is possible. It is at the soul, where my healing work with people occurs. Within the realm of this most pure and perfect energy, many results have been astounding.

The key is to attain the soul level. To reach this, we need to access the higher vibrational levels of energy through our essence, read the soul and heal ourselves. Our deepest pain dwells at the soul level. The soul needs to be healed, not because it is sick, as a soul never gets 'sick', but because it is incomplete and needs to be made whole. The physical body will have become impacted by an incomplete soul by exhibiting emotional distress or physical ailments, including cancer. When we link with our soul at the higher vibrational levels, our essence will encounter the most pure energy, which can heal us on all levels.

The body houses the sacred gift of the essence of the soul and should be kept as a temple, being honored by keeping it at optimum health. The soul is an exquisite creation. If the body is looked after at this viable level, it will remain on this Earth housing the essence to enable it to connect to the soul, so that the soul can continue to do its work here. When the soul becomes incomplete through the loss of a piece of energy due to trauma, attention should immediately be paid to make it whole again. This will prevent this deficit from translating into serious health issues of the brain and body.

An appropriate analogy of this situation is to consider a car. It runs well until a part fails and is now missing in the overall operation. The car still runs, but not as smoothly and it is a matter of time before the car engine will seize up or become almost inoperable. This analogy relates to the soul. With one or two pieces missing, we can continue to function and to live our life, but not as well. With numerous pieces missing and as all the issues begin to manifest in the physical level, the body will become, in time, physically 'inoperable'.

My spiritual journeys over eight years involved intensive work to raise the energy vibration by raising my frequency level, thereby shifting my energy density to be able to transmit the higher dimension energy of the 12th level of the energy plane. Most practitioners call on energies from the 1st to the 7th dimensions. I needed to access a higher and purer vibration to be able to do soul work effectively and help those people, who were dealing with serious issues in their life.

Each person has at least one missing energy piece of their soul and the majority of people have several missing pieces. The missing pieces are from traumatic events in the current and past lives. My work evolved into retrieving the missing energy of the soul by identifying the causal issues. By healing the energy of the soul and inspiring the spiritual, mental and physical levels to accept this, healing of their life could then begin. Retrieving a missing piece of soul energy is conducted in three phases: to locate and welcome the piece, to receive the piece and to accept the piece. During a healing consult, this piece of energy of the soul is shown to me as a short video of an event involving the person, at the age when the incident occurred. When I share this information with the person, they can recognize it very easily and add insights. Emotions will be released and a deep hurt brought to the surface to be eliminated. A Soul

Healing of the person would then be conducted to reunite the piece with their soul, to be received by the soul. The person is given instruction on how to now accept this piece into their soul. This must be conducted on their own, as it must come from their freewill to want this. With their undertaking towards attaining a complete soul, they can focus on retrieving other pieces at a later date. With even a single piece retrieved, a person's resolve to start truly living becomes inspirational.

It is a demanding task to focus on our inner soul when we are being bombarded with external information from all around us. Information is evident in the form of a television playing or a music player or a person speaking. When we listen to this type of information, our understanding comes wholly from our senses perceiving it and being processed through the brain. Information is less obvious when it is in the form of energy. When we get that 'gut feeling' and wish to know the message from the universe, we can 'listen' with our soul. These messages from a higher plane are processed in our spiritual level by the soul. To obtain these messages, we have to bypass the brain and access the soul level. This is done by allowing white light to enter the crown chakra at the top of the head. As the pure white light drifts down through the head, the neck and into the body, it will form a white sphere at the center within you, at the essence. This white light, like an activation switch, transmits to our spiritual level, connecting our essence with our soul at the higher level. This is the level at which the messages can be received in the form of energy. This explains why we question where this information is coming from, examining whether we actually did perceive it and even doubting the information, since it did not come to us in the usual manner.

Just as a person is able to communicate in more than one language, so listening to messages from the spiritual realm is merely another language of communication. We need to accept that we can learn this language and be competent to communicate with it.

We know how to access the information we need in our daily life. When we wake up from sleep, we usually want to know what time it is. Our life is determined by time since we need to know whether it is 3:00 a.m. and we can continue sleeping, or it is 6:30 a.m. and we need to get up to get ready for work. Time is necessary to bring many people together at the same interval, so even if we wish to ignore it, we must adhere to it. In the endeavor to access the information of time, we might initially guess what time it might be. Our guess is only confirmed when we look at the clock. What information would we have to gather to determine the time before we looked at the clock? Perhaps we know what month of the year it is and how much daylight there is; how tired we are and whether we have had enough sleep. Even if we pulled together all this information, the chances of knowing the exact time would be rare. Why is that? Why can we not simply ask what time it is and hear the answer, from the universe, not the spouse! We could, in fact, ask as those answers are around us.

Many people experience waking up in the middle of the night, looking at the clock and seeing a particular time, which has special meaning for them. It could be meaningful in several ways, but the usual significance is that it is the exact time a loved one passed away. This phenomenon comes under the umbrella of the term 'synchronicity', coined by psychologist Carl Jung, explaining such incidents are 'meaningful coincidences'. From my own experiences, I have found that the synchronicity occurs between the alpha and theta brain wave sections of sleep, during hypnagogia, when the energy is more susceptible to linking our spirit with the spiritual realm and receiving such information. It is just an acknowledging message to us that the person, who passed away at that time, is around us, watching out for us. Although this 'hello' is very welcome, it has sometimes come from them at 3:00 a.m. in the morning, as this was the time our mind was most receptive to this link.

If we think merely from the mechanism of the brain, our answers and solutions will be limited to its capacity. If we think outside of our body, our answers and solutions will be limitless and as infinite as the universe. Our reality will take on a new form. We will sense a new liberation when we open ourselves up to thinking outside of our body. Meditation is one method of being outside our body. During meditation, we can depart our physical level and encounter a separate reality. What this separate reality comprises, depends on what we need to be shown in order to heal.

Dreams are also a separate reality. There are dreams and there are journeys, which we undertake during the night. The difference between the two is that in a dream the brain is cataloging, whereas in the journey, the soul travels to learn by going through action, rather than just perceiving it. This information can then be acquired from the soul, by linking to it with the essence through the spiritual level, thereby bringing it into our life. You can further tell the difference from a dream, by noticing these aspects of a journey: there are usually a lot of people around; some of these people might be your family members, who have passed on; the sequence endures for quite a while; it is logical; you communicate with the people and they with you. The tool of the journey is very powerful. We are convinced the experience of the dream or journey is our reality until we wake up and ascertain the reality of our awake state to be true. Both realities can co-exist, but the key is to establish which reality we are in and that a reality is not of our own making.

Journeys will take us to the spiritual realm, the universe. It is a reality within that realm. It is also the 'other side', where we will go after our life ends. There are buildings, dwellings, gardens filled with vibrantly colored flowers and people. Its perfection is breathtaking. Until I exchange my experiences with another person who has had the same experience of journeying to the spiritual realm, I do not know whether that reality is what I alone see, or that same reality can be seen by everyone who journeys there. We can be continuously present in the earthly realm, but can only be briefly present in the spiritual realm while we live on Earth.

Working with energy is simply choosing in which reality to be present. Meditative images, dreams and journeys are energy. Information is converted into energy and then delivered to a person's spiritual level. When this is received, it is changed from that energy to a level of understanding and sometimes, parts are lost in translation, resulting in the fact that one or two portions do not make total sense. This is due to the fact that we persist in routing the information to the physical brain, which not only filters it but determines its validity, changes it to suit itself or discards some parts. Directing it to be received in the soul, maintains the integrity and truthfulness of the information to be used to inspire and heal us. Practising at directing the energy of the information to its end target, the soul, helps augment the integrity of the information.

I am able to remember most of my dreams clearly because these are stored in part in my brain and in part in my spiritual level. Although I can remember the journeys at night, they are not lodged in my brain but held entirely in my soul and the soul has a very different and wholesome way of preserving and recalling these experiences.

An example of one such journey will illustrate this clearly. One night, I experienced a journey. In the marbled halls of a building, I met a young man about eighteen years old, in a t-shirt and swim trunks wearing a medal for swimming on a ribbon. He told me he was very proud of his achievement. We talked and I understood there was an unresolved issue. Next day, asking various people if they recognized him did not bring about any results. I, my brain, concluded this young man had passed on at age eighteen and I had met his soul.

I could do no further work for him until I sent a Christmas email to a friend, who responded with wishes and added that he had been busy with his son's illness. The journey flooded back, but I was confused as I knew his son was thirty-five years old, although I had never met him. I asked my friend if his son had been a swimmer at school. He confirmed this. I asked if he had won any medals and was told that he had not.

Two things were now clear: my friend's son was still on this earth; I learned that I could connect with the soul of a living person I did not personally know. After reading the energy at soul level of the journey, I understood that the reason I had met this young man at eighteen was to understand a traumatic event, the death of someone close, which had happened in his life at that age. I asked my friend.

He told me his son had, in fact, won a medal for swimming and was very proud of it and he himself did not even know this had happened. He recounted the traumatic event, which had happened to his son at age eighteen and had affected him and two families. His son was driving a vehicle filled with students from their school graduation celebration when the car lost control, flipped over and one boy in the rear passenger seat died. My friend's son carried this huge burden until it manifested into cancer that Christmas.

I later connected with the young man who had died, who only wished well for his friend, did not blame him and wanted him to release the tremendous burden so that both their souls could be freed from this. When a soul has energy spaces as a result of trauma, that piece must be identified and reunited or the person cannot move on in life and will repeat the same disappointing cycles. People trapped in these cycles usually encounter cancer or other debilitating diseases. This phenomenon has contributed to the increased incidence of these diseases. When the soul is complete, the person can heal and move on in their life.

Communications and healings for my friend's son spanned several weeks. I conducted several remote Healings of Release and Soul Healings and today, he is cancer free. To this day, I have never met my friend's son. The power of the journey showed me the issue of a person in distress. The power of the soul showed me how truly amazing and limitless it is in delivering healing.

Following that experience, and having been made aware that I could connect during a journey with the soul of a living person I did not personally know, I had a memorable encounter. I went on a journey and saw a Hollywood actor walking up to me. I recognized him, but I will not disclose his name since private details of his life were revealed to me. I will call him Mike. Over the next few weeks, we would participate in four journeys, talking and sharing like friends. During the last journey, we walked with linked arms, discussing his upcoming marriage in two months. He expressed his apprehension to get married although she was a lovely young lady. This would not be his first marriage and he was uneasy. He did not wish another failure to play out in social media and on tv. I listened and suggested that he be truthful to his fiancé and cancel the wedding if this is what they both decided. Stopping the wedding was in his heart, but the outcome of the fear of disappointing his fiancé and other celebrity wedding guests, and the spiteful portrayal in social media was preventing him from cancelling. He told me he would go ahead with the wedding. When I woke up, it was much to my chagrin that I had to recount to my husband, that I was walking with a very handsome Hollywood actor, and we were discussing the issues of his life! My husband simply laughed! This supposedly illustrates the inability to manipulate journeys!

Mike did go through with the wedding. The marriage lasted three years and they divorced. During the marriage, I did not share a journey with Mike, but after the divorce, we shared one more journey. My role was as a listener, as he confided in me about the heartbreaking events of his life in the public eye during and after the divorce. He was saddened to have had to endure the very circumstance that he had tried to avoid. We talked about finding the truth and courage in his soul to make the best decisions for himself and those close to him. He understood he should not store the fear of other people's opinions and allow this to determine his choices.

The experience of these journeys with Mike inspires the curiosity, should I have the pleasure of meeting him, whether I would seem familiar to him. I hold the hope that he will feel a kinship without fully understanding why! I do, however, fully understand that this is most likely my brain directing this thought, not my soul!

Sometimes a dream can have another reality within it. I often have a dream and refer to it in the next night's dream. This can further be compacted into a dream within a dream. I had a dream about a person. I believed that I had woken up to tell them about the dream, but then realized that this in itself was a dream encapsulated in the first dream. While being present in the dream, both dreams were a reality to me. This can certainly increase the confusion of which reality we are living.

Energy can sometimes send us a message through an object. This was shown to me in the example of a bunch of red roses a friend received. They were accepted fresh, but the next day, they were withered. Within two days, this represented the end of the relationship between my friend and the man who gave her the roses. Similar signs are all around us and we need to notice them, then to heed them. Signs can be in the form of a change in the feeling of the air around us. I have coined the term 'atmosphere' to describe this. This atmosphere can give an excitement in the air or bring certain emotions to the surface within us. All these signs are forewarnings of an event, positive or challenging, to prepare us to incorporate it into our life in the best way possible.

Our own energy is comprised of: the energy within us, the energy accessed by our soul and the new energy we introduce through our crown chakra, all operating at different frequencies. There is an overlap of two dynamics, where the energy of the brain's thoughts and the soul's experiences are each modulating at a different frequency. Hence it is an ordeal to traverse fluidly from the brain to the soul and link with the messages of the soul. Since energy is not contained solely within our physical body, so our health issues are also not contained exclusively within the body. Our emotional, mental and physical issues have infiltrated our soul and are no longer accessible from the mental or physical level. To resolve this, we need to access the energy from beyond us at the higher levels. Although it is an ordeal, it is not impossible to accomplish. This process will be described in a later chapter.

Our individual energy is analogous to the next person's, yet dissimilar enough to create our own unique energy. Consequently, working with energy using one method might be successful for one person, but may lack effectiveness for another. We have to determine which method works best for us and then work it with our energy. In my healing work, as well as getting to know the person's personality, I also have to get to know the 'personality' of their energy and customize my healing accordingly, which I do in real time throughout the entire healing session.

Just as our energy is unique to each one of us, so is our physical appearance. We each have a face with eyes, a nose, a mouth, ears, so, by definition, we should all look identical. Even though we each have the same features, each face is distinct from another face, as a result of a different shape, size and color. Each face takes on its own individuality. Hence, we are able to recognize people. What a world it would be if we all had identical faces! The differences in facial features are subtle enough to present individuality but prominent enough to produce a variance. This variance in facial features has given great success to the facial recognition programs used by law enforcement, identifying and locating malicious people to prevent potential harm to others.

Despite being born in different countries around the world and with diverse expectations in life, human beings have a foundation of comparable emotions. We all know how special love is, that we can feel happy and smile, that we feel sad and cry tears and that we can become nervous or scared. Emotions have not been taught to us. Every single person has the innate triggers within us to produce these emotions in given situations. Our individuality is exhibited by how we deal with the emotions.

3
My background

My journey of appreciating the energy around me has spanned my entire life. I was using energy before I recognized I was using it. I have never known anything different. It is as intrinsic in me as the fibre of my body. I attribute this to maintaining a connection with my triplet sister after she passed away as a baby. We were part of each other while she was alive and now we are part of each other through energy.

My earliest recollection of instinctively using energy on myself was at age six, after a traumatic incident in my life, which affected my soul. I was at school in the country where I grew up. It was at a time when a teacher had the ultimate and unquestioning authority. The discipline of children could be enforced with physical punishment. Today, this would be totally unacceptable and even termed abuse, not discipline. In the context of my early time at school, it was accepted as discipline, although the devastating effects on a child physically and emotionally could still be enormous.

My classmates and I were being trained to use an ink fountain pen. This seems inconceivable nowadays, to give a six-year-old child liquid ink, but that was the era. I put in all my effort to round each letter. To my horror, I saw, in slow motion, a blob of dark blue ink sliding down the nib. Before I could think to move the pen away from the notebook, the blob hit the page and spluttered upwards, then landed across the width of two lines of my page. My heart began to pound. I used the corner of the blotting paper to blot the excess ink. In my peripheral vision, I caught the huge form of the senior teacher lumbering towards me, so I moved my arm to shield my work. As she stood behind me, she grabbed my arm and jerked it aside to get a better view. To the tempo of her words admonishing me for the untidy work, she hit the back of my skull with her open palm several times. My tiny form fell forward with each stroke. I understood she was commanding me to go and wash out the pen. I went into the school bathrooms and sobbed very hard. Not only had my body been hurt, but my soul had also been profoundly wounded. I stopped sobbing suddenly. Even at age six, my instinct was to separate my body and spirit, so that the pain and hurt could not take hold and spread recklessly through my body. I closed my eyes and saw white light around me. I breathed deeply and calmly. I have retained the ability to do this and use it as a protective shield. I told no one about this occurrence at school, but as a six-year-old child, I still had to find a way to deal with it on my own. My abilities in healing may have been awakened at that time when I recognized I myself needed healing.

My siblings and I were ostracized by the other school children, as our parents were not of the pure origin of that country. This placed me in the situation of an observer, whether I wanted this or not. I had always felt 'different', although not understanding why. I put this down to having a different background, but the dissimilarity extended beyond this; I saw people and things uniquely; I could see past the outer shell of their body. Only twenty-five years later, would I begin to understand what exactly it was that I was doing; I was seeing their soul. I was seeing images with my 'third eye', using my sixth sense. The third eye is an energy center located between our eyebrows, which has the ability to see the spiritual realm after a person has chosen to open it. I used the alienation I encountered and the abuse by a teacher as a catalyst to healing myself and then, later in my life, to bring healing to others.

My early childhood was challenging, comprising of feelings of not being wanted by the society in which we lived and of not having close friends at school. My parents were loving and embracing, working very hard to provide for us and to make our life as tolerable as possible. The schools and the neighbors did not offer any kind of support. My family and I had to spend a great deal of time focusing on maintaining basic necessities, but there was still some opportunity for me to explore freeing the mind. My vantage point as an outsider was a blessing, not a hardship, as it enabled me to observe people and objects. As I grew up, I had to learn to bridge the gap of observing the energy around, yet still be involved in daily life. The spiritual realm became that link and the balance came into being. I could access the spiritual realm from the conscious state, so did not have to do this at night, while falling asleep. I could receive information from the spiritual realm while going about my daily life. In actuality, I had the best of both realms, whenever

I wanted. In my childhood, I did not realize this was what was happening, but in my adulthood, I learned that access to very valuable knowledge from the spiritual realm had been present in my life for as long as I could remember.

I was able to do mind gymnastics as a child. I was able to visualize items, places or people without ever having seen them. I could read the energy of a person's emotions. Since I did this at night, I assumed it was part of a dream, resulting in these abilities becoming buried and forgotten. When I began reading books about the spiritual realm, I was not learning new information, but in fact, re-wakening those same gifts. I credit some of my gift to my mother, who had great spiritual awareness and would casually mention things without going into any depth.

School in the senior grades continued to have its challenges. I had never been totally assimilated, nor did I feel part of a large, accepting group, but in spite of this, I made the best of it. I had one or two very close friends in the later grades and we shared good times together. I successfully passed all the exams necessary for university entrance. The rejection felt during my years at school transformed into absorbing more knowledge from the spiritual realm, without being aware of this. It became second nature. Over the years, I have never had to learn about matters of the energy beyond us; I just had to discover it. This is true for us all. We all have the intuition for this. This ability has always been with you, if only you knew how to tap into it.

As I evolved spiritually, I read books and was open to attending classes on the subject. I listened to what the presenter had to say, but only accepted those aspects which resonated totally with me. Since I already had a foundation of spiritual awareness, I needed the knowledge to expand this and not to introduce new concepts which contradicted this. Although our spiritual evolvement might overlap with another's experience to some extent, it is still unique to us and as individual as we are.

As a probable consequence of the ostracization I experienced at school, I began to feel that I was performing as if in a theater play each role I was undertaking in life. I played the part of a school student, then a university student, a person seeking employment, a traveller to another country and throughout this I was encountering people, who were also acting a part. This gave me the awareness that the body is merely an enclosure to enable this performance. The body is a temporary containment of our actions, emotions, reactions, so we can, therefore, be fully aware of when our thoughts extend beyond this. When we understand the role-playing here on Earth, it makes absolute sense that the minor irritations, which we accumulate during our day, should not matter in the bigger scheme of things. I am human; the same things that bother you, bother me: the heavy traffic making me late for an appointment, no empty parking spot outside the grocery store, being overcharged at a store. Each day, I try to minimize the importance of such concerns. I put them into perspective, by holding them up into the framework of the bigger scheme and usually find that to attribute importance to them is not warranted. I have more significant items with which to concern myself.

I hear conversations around me, displaying the positive or negative interaction of two people. I see clearly the role playing and can, therefore, become detached from it, as it is only playing, after all. This is not to minimize the events of our life, as these have great value, but to put into perspective the minor frustrations for being what they are. We spend time in role playing this way on Earth until it is time to leave and take our lessons with us.

My quest to learn more about healing began in a traditional manner of aspiring to learn about medicine. Seventeen years ago, I began an adult student course in medicine at the local university. I had never intended to enter the profession of a physician in allopathic medicine, but the information intrigued me. The reason for learning this knowledge would make itself evident years later, when, during a healing, I saw the blackened energy of a vital organ, signifying that it was under duress and was able to recognize which organ it was. At the end of the medical course, one of the final lectures addressed alternative medicine and Reiki energy. I was captivated.

Since I am a proponent of the phrase, 'there are no coincidences', I had to smile when, the next day, I turned on the television, which was showing a program about Reiki Energy. I began watching. During this program, I learned the reason why my hands always emitted a lot of heat. I was very excited about this topic and explored local courses in Reiki Healing. I undertook a two-year course and earned the accreditation of Reiki Master Healer.

My learning did not stop there, as I now had a great motivation to pursue other healing modalities. Earning a certification in Feng Shui grew out of my belief that healing a person had an implied limited success rate if they returned to an environment, which had sick energy, and they re-absorbed it. I blended the two modalities to facilitate a total healing for a person and their environment, which became Feng Shui Healing. It further evolved into a blend of various healing modalities and pure energy from the universe. Since no name existed for this, I named it

'Soul Life Healing'. From this, my practice was created. The evolution of my healing work, however, continued, as I was beginning to explore Soul Healing.

From all this learning grew the awareness that if a person carried deep pain, this had to be released if the healing of their life was to be total. If the deeply embedded pain within their soul could heal, this would enable healing at the spiritual level and result in bringing healing to the physical level. Endeavoring to study more about the soul, I learned Shamanic Healing during my own personal journeys. This period of learning spanned eight years but, in some ways, it has evolved throughout my whole life. With the incorporation of Soul Healing into my healing method eight years ago, my work has advanced with great intensity.

I now knew my path in life and the work I was to do. We each search for our purpose and fulfillment. This might stem from the desire to be useful in our life or to discover the meaning of living a life. Many years ago, I asked God to show me my calling. What was I on this Earth to do? I received my answer and I never expected the journey I would take and the growth and beauty it would bring. The pathway of healing was unfolded before me in manageable steps, gentle guidance and a fulfillment in my soul.

I am not a Healer; I bring Healing. I bring the information for healing from a realm of energy beyond us. People have a variety of names for where this comes from, Source, Universe, Light. For me, it is God. The healing comes from God. I would really like to take the credit for some astounding healings at which I have been present, but I am merely the vessel, the link, as only God can realize these incredible achievements. I am, however, humbled to be a part of it and proud that I am capable of receiving the information which can help people.

With the evolvement of sharing my work with people seeking to be healed, I encountered the huge challenge which had its roots in my childhood. The early experience of school, the ostracization and the ridicule had resulted in the total absence of my confidence in front of other people. This had a twofold impact on my career goal and my healing consults.

I always wanted to have a career as a teacher, which was being threatened by my lack of confidence. Despite the despicable example of the teacher I had at six years old, this was an attractive vocation to me. Only in my senior year of school, when I had to embark on applying to teacher training colleges, did I realize that teaching in the traditional capacity of a school teacher was not my goal. I felt certain that the universe would provide a unique blend of how I would teach many people in a distinct way. Teaching, or more precisely guidance, is a part of the work I do today and I greatly enjoy it.

For me to be effective during healing consults, I would have to face the issue of limited confidence. I found myself being placed in situations, where these fears would surface. There was the option to face the fears or run away from them. I could not run away from my fears, as I had to be in front of a person, communicate with them and share my healing ability. Trust would only be instilled in them if I exhibited confidence in my demeanor and in my information. Although this was extremely difficult for me to do, I propelled forward, driven by the objective to help people heal. Throughout this, grueling as it was, I put aside my human fears and put faith and trust at the forefront and left it to a higher power. This was the journey of my own healing. I worked on myself before I would allow myself to work with others. Through healing and journeys, my confidence was revitalized in me, more extensive than I could ever have imagined. Today, I observe people, for whom I have brought healing, living happier and more fulfilled lives. Having reclaimed my confidence, I now also give presentations and teach sessions to large groups about improving their lives. Anything is possible.

I do not profess to be privy to knowledge never before spoken. I am just an open vessel to it. This openness makes me trust the information I receive and to be able to pass it on confidently to the person in front of me during a healing session. Their astonished reaction validates the information as accurate and poignant for them. It was a lengthy process of sixteen years to reach the spiritual point, where I felt I had valuable information to share. When I am in a healing consult with a person, I am able to visualize their homes, their family members alive and passed, issues from their childhood or facing them presently, because they bring this energy with them. This is the baggage they carry. This energy generates the visualization for me to see the images of what is affecting them. I then describe this to them and elicit responses which help them consider an issue in a different light. Receiving healing energy will then guide them to a resolution.

I spend weeks preparing for a public presentation, fine tuning it so that it will be the best possible information for my audience and that it is complete at the time of delivery. Although I receive inspiration for the material, I am in control of the total content. This is very different from the way in which I receive information and messages for a client. During deep thought, I am given twenty-five percent of the information during about two hours in the evening prior to a client consult the next day. Only one consult per day is scheduled so that I can be totally dedicated to only that person on that day. Were two people to be scheduled on the same day, there would not be the risk of confusion of information, as the spiritual realm is not prone to confusion. I have made allowances in extenuating circumstances for people wishing to travel together to have consults on the same day. I prefer, however, to honor that one person by dedicating myself to only them on that day. I further commit two hours prior to their arrival in preparation of the energy in the room, my energy and the selection of the music. Although the person sits in front of me for up to one and a quarter hours, the entire healing process spans five hours.

Not being in possession of one hundred percent of the information for the client makes me apprehensive, as I feel ill-prepared. I would like to be totally organized for my consults. Just prior to the healing, my personal thoughts are put to one side, so that I can become a totally blank channel, able to receive the client's information. At the consult, I receive the balance of the information during the interaction with the client and during the Soul Healing. Spirit has asked me to have faith and trust that I will receive all the essential information to pass on to the person and provide them with the optimum healing. To deliver the information spontaneously could be stressful, but I have learned to trust that the healing will be the best healing for the person. This is, in fact, how it does work every time and the most astonishing information occurs spontaneously during the consult. This information does not come through my brain but directly through my soul. I feel the information downloaded to my soul, but I use my mouth to transfer this into words for the person to hear. I think of it as the impromptu part of the healing consult. I am unaware of what I will say until I hear myself actually saying it. Other than the Soul Healing, it is typically the most dramatic and startling part of the consult. This also makes each healing unique; no two healing consults are remotely similar.

Usually, a person will not attend a healing with just one minor issue. There are typically numerous issues present, some being deeply entrenched and some being interlocked with each other. A person will achieve a rudimentary level of healing for one or two of their issues. Healings will build, one upon the other, and advance the healing until total healing is achieved. Each healing consult is an independent unit and a contributory building block to the entire healing process. The more often a person attends a healing consult, the more rapidly the advance is made towards total healing.

I am able to read a person's energy remotely over the phone, but I prefer to see their face, not so I can read their expressions, but so they will sense a connection of energy with me. Once I have met with a person or have seen them face-to-face, then it is no problem, if the need arises, to do a healing for them remotely without needing to see them. They do not have to be present or even aware that I am doing a healing for them.

I had a very remarkable experience of the power of remote healing. After a consult with a client, I felt prompted to email her the next day to tell her to be aware of her blood pressure. She was not currently experiencing a BP issue. She advised that she would use her friend's BP arm band monitor. The next day, she experienced a greatly elevated BP and was ready to go to the hospital, but emailed me for my help. It was no coincidence that I was on my computer when the email arrived, so I was immediately able to help. I did a remote healing to release her anxiety and brought pure energy to lower her BP. One hour later, she emailed to advise that her BP was normal and thanked me. Even I was quite amazed that this positive result was so instantaneous. It was the power of energy at its most impressive.

My work is Energy: energy within the physical body, within the home, within the mind, within the spiritual level and within the soul. I work with a unique blend of several modalities and higher vibrational levels of energy, which are attuned to a person's specific needs to bring them healing and release. It is a powerful energy fusion. I have formulated a synthesis of Reiki, Cosmic, Mahatma, Quantum, Universal, Shamanic and my own innovations. I have now been involved in Energy Healing for thirty years, and with my healing practice for the past seventeen years.

My spiritual evolution has mostly developed in a predetermined manner. Now and again, events happen which surprise me. A few years ago, I awoke to see two people in my bedroom. This was unsettling to awaken and see this, but I did have enough awareness that these were of the spirit world. This occurred for several continuous nights, the largest group being four. They were always respectful and would stand far away from me. I understood that these were souls, who had crossed over but had left something unfinished and were seeking my assistance to mediate to complete it. I knew that, from the healing work I do, that I have white light around me and they had been drawn to this. I asked God that, if this were to be a part of my work to heal souls who had recently crossed, then I would do this. I could not, however, awaken to seeing them in front of me and have my heart pounding in my throat. No more souls came that same way. I now journey to the other side and meet souls, both passed and living, within an exquisite building made of white marble. There I can hear their issue and help them resolve their unfinished matter. These souls are connected with future clients or familiar people, whom I am able to reach.

My spiritual development is directed for me with incredible purpose and intention. I am being allowed to journey, visiting buildings in heaven, meeting with souls there and receiving instruction and understanding of the larger realm. This is all done on heaven's time-table and initiative, not mine. If I were to determine when and where in heaven to travel, I would be there all the time and explore as much as I could. This is why I have no fear of death, as this is where I would ultimately be. I presently have the optimum situation of being able to visit heaven, yet return to bring the information to share in a healing for a person, resulting in a healthier and happier life for them.

Although my guidance from the universe has been ongoing for seventeen years, I am still learning and still evolving. I never cease to be impressed with what is shown to me to allow me to learn. The guidance is always with tiny yet distinct steps, and I am always shown patience so that I reach a particular level of understanding before proceeding to the next. I am drawn to Tibetan healing, wisdom, chants and knowledge, so I have been given a guide who has Ancient Wisdom, which is shared with me. All my guides have certainly fulfilled their role as the best teachers, turning my ears into eyes.

This is a western society in which I live, so I cannot totally discount western traditional medicine, nor do I wish to. I have every respect for the medical profession since this is where my own path began in learning about medicine. If I were to live in China or Japan, a greater proportion of healing of a person would be energy or holistic healing, since those countries are more accepting of these methods. Their populations have grown up being surrounded by this knowledge and these countries have incorporated it into their healthcare system. Western hospitals have medical specialists and although this appears to be beneficial in that they know absolutely everything about a small area of the body or an organ, they will treat only that area with no intention of causing a negative impact in other areas of the body. I chose to direct my work to look at the source of an ailment, be it on the physical or emotional level, then to deal with that, eradicating it through the spiritual level to bring improved health. By virtue of my work, it is impossible for me to treat a symptom and not the cause. The soul always holds the cause. Soul Healing differs in its effectiveness from allopathic medicine, as it can target the cause of an ailment, without needing to discover the cause, as it will be presented to the healer. Traditional medicine requires discovery and knowledge of the cause to bring effective treatment of the symptom. This is challenging in conventional medicine, as, for example, if the symptom were to be abdominal pain, this could be a myriad of causes. Time and money would be spent on tests, with no assurance that the cause would even be discovered. When the cause is established by the doctors, treatment would then occur based on that premise.

My healing work will never end. There is so much healing needed to be done and enough healing to create a great deal of work for all of us. There are not enough healers in the world. This is almost a contradiction of terms, as each one of us has the potential to be an outstanding healer for ourselves and for others.

I am questioned during my healing consults or during presentations, mostly out of interest and to gain a fuller understanding. My theories are my own. I welcome all the questions since, by having to give the answers to the questioner, I am also being given the answers for myself. They can question away because I myself did. I questioned every step of my journey. I scrutinized everything, wanting to know and understand its origins. I questioned each development for six years, until I finally heard, "Now Trust. Now have Faith". There is no stipulation for a person to believe in my abilities, but just to believe in the abilities of God and that I am merely an instrument.

I am so enthusiastic, leaping at an opportunity to help people, that this is sometimes perceived as being readily available. The receiver might, therefore, discount the true value of my fervor and take it for granted. In this way, they could potentially miss the immense value of the gift. I had to learn to handle this by requesting that people, who truly respected the gift, to be sent to me.

Not only have I undertaken a journey to learn about my gift in the traditional institutions and also the spiritual level, but I have simultaneously accomplished my own healing. I practise what I preach. The information and tools that I share with people, I myself use them, in my life and in my healing work. I am a testament that healing and empowering the soul do work; I have a tremendous husband/friend, three children who are accomplished and pleasant people to know, excellent family health, my healing work is fulfilling and I have a beautiful home. I like my life and I am happy. It is more than being happy, as I can truly feel the happiness.

I am pleased that these key elements of my life are flourishing, but I am also happy with the small but wonderful traces of happiness in my day of sitting on the patio with my husband, seeing the exquisite colors of a sunrise or having my cat jump up for a cuddle. Being happy does not mean that I will not encounter challenges in my life. I will. It does mean, however, that I will have the resilience and be adequately equipped to handle them and eradicate them before they can fester into other areas of my life. I want to and need to have challenges in my life as my soul has to evolve.

4
The ways to access energy

Once we have accepted the notion of the existence of energy around us, we can master the techniques to access it. We need to understand the basics of energy, but not in the sense of physics. Everything is energy. Energy, known as Chi or Qi in Eastern cultures, constitutes our body, our pets, our furniture, our cell phones, our monetary notes and food. Everything. The energy within our body and around us is vital to the wellbeing of our life.

This energy has a range of vibrations, modulating at different levels, affected by the various influences of heat, electricity, the presence of a particular color, whether a window or door is in close proximity or whether articles are strewn on the floor. When these varied vibrational energies unite, it changes the area, sometimes positively and sometimes negatively. In order to mitigate the negative consequence of the energy, we can strategically place items or colors with the ultimate goal to transform this energy into lighter energy to flow more easily. This lighter energy can then nourish that area of our environment and thereby, the corresponding element of our life. The modality of Feng Shui is based on this concept.

There are several weights of energy, which come together to form an object, furniture, walls, fabric, our body, everything. The energy weight bands are irregularly interspersed within the object, some being thicker than others. If this variety of strata could be extracted and grouped like with like, the bands would display a graduation from pure, light and fast energy to thick, heavy and slow energy. The heavy energy, which does not flow well within our body or environment, causes us issues in our health and life. Theoretically, it would be a simple task to identify only the unwanted heavy energy, extract and eliminate it. These bands are, however, totally amalgamated, so the entire object must be treated as a unity. The optimum goal would be to achieve one single layer comprised of the highest, the lightest and the fastest energy. This is impossible to attain, due to the constantly changing environmental influences, so we are subjected to work with it as is and aim for the best practical result.

The importance of energy cannot be understated. Take, for example, a car. It is energy. Would it not be beneficial if the energy was of the lightest consistency so that when two cars met in a road intersection, they would simply pass 'through' each other, rather than be thick energy and collide with each other, causing injury to the occupants? This might be somewhat futuristic but is merely being presented as an analogy of the efficacy of energy.

Observing and working with energy over the years, my work has brought me to the point where I can read the energy in strata and readily identify the thicker energy. I would then cleanse these lower heavy, thick layers. This is achieved by removing obstructions or stagnant energy from the thicker layers, thereby making them lighter, whereby they will drift upward and be incorporated into the upper lighter band.

In a body, the lower, thick bands are not necessarily at our feet. These thicker layers would be located throughout the body at the points where there is a health issue present or a potential one. Energy in a sentient body is more complex than the energy in an item. Within the multiple energy layers of a body, there is a range of lighter to heavier energy. This strata composition is distinctive, as it additionally has its own unique bands of emotional, mental and physical energy within each layer. Due to this complexity, the energy of our body is read as separate layers for each of the physical, emotional or mental levels. Each level can be treated separately and a particular issue could then be targeted.

The energy of our body intermingles with the energy of the environment we inhabit. This results in our body absorbing both positive and negative energy from our surroundings, so it is crucial to keep the energy in our home and workplace pure and cleansed. If we do not attend to keeping pure energy within us, it will manifest in detrimental ways in our body and we will suffer ailments or be forced to look after issues physically with pharmaceutical medications or surgery. As an example, a person, who has absorbed the energy within themselves which causes them to rely continually on others for all their needs and decisions, may have leg issues or multiple sclerosis. Symbolically, this would be that this person cannot stand on their own two feet. If this energy is not extracted through healing, renewed and regenerated, this condition will exacerbate, causing further degeneration of the person's body.

In our home, certain rooms contain a great deal of heavy energy; bathrooms, for obvious reasons of having to expel waste. The energy of drains, waste pipes and used towels generated in the bathroom does not contain itself there and, if allowed to infiltrate the rest of the house, major areas of the inhabitants' lives will be adversely affected. Whether it perhaps has its roots in ancient Feng Shui knowledge, I have encountered several instances while conducting Feng Shui Healing in a home, where the energy of a bathroom has negatively affected the brains, thought processes and emotions of teenage boys. It is therefore recommended that a boy's bed in his room is not located underneath or above a bathroom.

In our body and our homes, we sometimes have a 'bubble' of energy. As a bubble, this is waiting to burst. This is not a pleasant image, but then this is not a pleasant circumstance. Since no clearing of energy has occurred over a long period of time, the thick and stuck energy has been allowed to accumulate to form this huge bubble. When the bubble reaches a large size, it will burst, radiating sticky energy in all directions. This will infiltrate all areas of the environment, representing all elements of our life. This thick energy requires dispelling to lighten its weight and enable it to begin flowing again, thus mitigating the menacing effects on elements of our life.

Compounded with this, is the unfavorable impact of the energy of a mirror. People have many mirrors decorating the walls of their home. A mirror should be placed with a very specific purpose, for example, the bathroom mirror, which has the purpose of letting you see yourself as you wash your face, comb your hair or apply makeup. A mirror should be placed and used in the house with a purpose, not as adornment. Without a specific purpose, a mirror creates a tunnel effect of spiralling energy and a depth that does not serve us well. The rudimentary energy of an item can be pulled into this spiral, absorbed into it, be itself spiralled and ejected. Spiralling energy, meandering through your home's energy, is a catastrophe waiting to happen. Until halted, this energy will continue to alter the energy in your home with cumulative intensity. This will ultimately affect your life adversely. Since this type of malevolent energy does not serve you, it is recommended to keep placement of mirrors to a minimum. Fortunately, our body's energy composition is too complex to be absorbed into the energy of a mirror but is still at risk to the energy emanating from the mirror.

Although natural light entering through windows is the ideal system, the light in our homes is provided to some extent by lightbulbs. Attention should be paid to any lamp bulbs which are not working and they should be immediately replaced. The energy of a faulty lightbulb is, very simply, giving you a warning. This warning is twofold; to get your attention for an imminent message; to address the thick, negative energy, which has damaged or popped the lightbulb. If it is a means to get your attention, you are to look out for a message intended to help you avoid or handle a problematic situation. You should, therefore, be aware of the occurrence of the next unusual event. If it is a case of thick energy, which has accumulated in that area, overwhelming the lightbulb and causing it to fail, a notation should be made of its location. The Feng Shui zone of your home or office, where the lightbulb is located, would correspond to that element of your life, which will be adversely affected. This hint is being displayed for you in a clear way, so it would be prudent to determine what it might concern and heed the warning.

Unlike a light bulb, a rupture in a water pipe or faucet has a detrimental effect no matter where it is located. Water is symbolic of money. Wasted water in a dripping tap or a running toilet tank becomes a loss of money. If a faucet hose or pipe were to burst, this would signify an unexpected expense, other than the cost to repair the issue. The energy of the water translates into effecting money. It is recommended to fix the issue immediately and clear the energy of the affected area to avoid a reoccurrence.

The energy strata of our entire home join together and form a nucleus at the center, which is the area which cannot be adjusted directly. This area can only be changed by fine-tuning the energy at the peripheries. This treatment is a combination of Feng Shui and Energy Healing. Once the energy at the outer borders is pure, light and flowing, the energy at the center will then come into balance. This is a crucial area of energy, as it represents the 'I', our health-giving life and our personal health.

Energy entering or moving through our environment can be equated to the ingredients of a recipe; if the ingredients are complete and the preparation is thorough, the result is a tasty meal. If an ingredient is missing or the cooking is poor, the end result is a meal, which might be barely edible, lacks taste, has limited nutrients and does not bring enjoyment to eat it. This is also true of the need to preserve the complete and positive elements of energy in our body, life, home and office, to give us the best opportunity for an agreeable life.

As an analogy of energy which does not serve us, imagine walking and unexpectedly finding yourself in smoke. Since your senses have the opportunity to become aware of this, you might gag and your instinct would signal you to get as far away as possible. Such is the energy which is harmful to us, but unfortunately, we do not sense it, so we continue to be in it, to live in it and to have it flowing through our body. I show people how to sense it, become aware of it, clear it and improve it.

It takes some practice to become aware of the energy in our home. A first step would be to become aware of the energy in our body. No one would question providing food and nutrients for our body, so why would we not supply healthy energy to our body? Bringing in new, vital energy will nourish the body. Just as we need food and water to sustain our bodies, so we need to take in pure energy to thrive spiritually. When we are healthy spiritually, at the soul level, we will be healthy physically, emotionally, mentally and be able to lead fulfilled lives. As well as attending to the energy in our body and environment, it is also advocated to bring the energy into the soul for healing. Herein lies the source of deep and true healing of our life. Soul Healing will be discussed in-depth in a later chapter.

Working with energy, directing it, changing it and regenerating it, is a delicate balance. For this reason, it is not advisable to introduce new energy into many zones of the home at the same time. People believe that, by adjusting all facets of their home's energy at the same time, the positive results will all materialize at the same time for them and promptly improve all aspects of their life. This is not so. The contrary result will materialize. There is a shift in energy when pure, new energy is introduced, so to allow so much simultaneous shifting causes the swirling of energy, flowing haphazardly in your home. Swirling could be compared to an outside wind blowing around leaves, agitating air in random directions. You would not sense any breeze in your home, so you would be unaware of this happening. Changing one layer at a time in a methodical manner is the optimal way to handle the adjustment of energy. A layer can be managed each day, allowing the energy to be introduced in a measured way and avoiding any swirling. Patience is still required to nurture the energy to achieve the desired results.

Energy can be enhanced through color, shapes and sound. Each color has a vibrational frequency. It is therefore recommended to place certain colors appropriately in your home or to wear them. The science of Feng Shui is based on introducing specific colors into particular areas of your home, which represent aspects of your life, thereby enhancing them.

Certain shapes are comprised of energy in a very concentrated form and carry a force of their own. Examples are a pyramid and cone. Pyramids are very powerful, not only due to their thousands of years of existence since the ancient Egyptian culture but also due to the vibration created by their intense shape, a solid foundation crowning in a fine peak. It is one of the most dominant shapes in existence. The cone is similar to the pyramid with its peak and functions like a megaphone, drawing in energy and making it more robust, strengthening it. The pyramid or cone can be used to funnel energy and focus it, bringing positive results to the object to which it is connecting.

Sounds each exist at a different frequency, each producing a unique effect on us. Tibetan Singing Bowls illustrate this. Each bowl, when sounded, plays a harmonic frequency, a note. This note equates to a chakra in our body and this is why it resonates with us. Seven chakras are represented by the seven notes of a music scale, A, B, C, D, E, F, G. Based on ancient Tibetan Buddhism, the third eye responds to the note of A, the crown chakra to the note of B, the root to that of C and so on.

Words are energy. Words also carry energy. You send them out while talking and this energy interacts with the energy of words spoken by another person, producing results, whether you desire these particular results or not. We can control this to some extent by placing the energy of words around us, which will generate a positive, light energy, by stating affirmative words such as, 'love', 'faith', 'compassion' and 'trust'. This energy will be created and flow around us. Conversely, if negative words are spoken, this will create negative energy around us and the person at whom they were directed.

Thoughts are energy. They come into being by the brain of a person, who creates them. Now they exist. I receive thoughts. I cannot read another's thoughts, as the thinker has not given permission for me to sense the energy of their thoughts. If this is required during a healing, I will be given their deep thoughts through spirit with the intended result that this will help bring them healing. By virtue of having a person sit with me in a healing, permission is understood, and a person becomes open to the exchange of revealing their thoughts and receiving guiding information.

Thoughts can be exchanged remotely. This is known as telepathy. Information, in the form of energy, can be sent remotely from one person to another. Both parties should be competent in understanding and recognizing energy for telepathy to succeed. Both parties must also consent to do this, to avoid the circumstance of one person attempting to read another's thoughts without their knowledge or permission.

With the tools of using color, shapes and sound, frequency can also be used to rebalance the energy in our environment. Crystals and stones have an energetic and vibrational nature and are utilized to generate a particular frequency if they are strategically placed in the home. These crystals and stones must be cleared and fine-tuned from time to time in order to maintain the delicate balance. I work with smoky quartz during a healing, clearing unhealthy energy from a person, while simultaneously receiving healing energy and messages of guidance. With this double duty, I can be more effective in retrieving more information for the person. Since it takes a lot of energy for souls to connect with us on the Earth plane, I use a crystal to transmit this energy more fluently, thus streamlining it and utilizing their energy more efficiently. Each person is drawn to the crystal which will work most positively for them. When the crystal is doing its job efficiently, it will become plugged with the thick energy it has collected and will require clearing. Consider it like vacuuming your home. When the vacuuming is done, it will last for a while but will need to be done again. Crystals can be cleared with running water, by leaving them in the light of a full moon or by making a verbal statement of clearing.

Animals have an innate sense of energy. They know where the positive and agreeable energy is in your home. They will choose to go there, even lying down and going to sleep, as it is so comfortable. Animals are also able to pick up energy from a great distance. When I go to a room in my house, my cat will show up there a short time after, even finding me on a different floor level. She can find me anywhere in the house without following me. She knows my energy, picks it up remotely and is drawn towards it. Birds are also drawn towards positive energy. Directly outside the room, where healings are conducted, is a lilac tree. Before a healing commences, there can be about two dozen chickadees, sparrows and finches who sit in that tree. They are attracted to the heightened pure energy in that room, just prior to a healing.

People usually need a little more evident information to attain similar results of knowing where good energy is. If a person were outside on a hot day and began to feel very hot and uncomfortable, they would probably choose to go into the shade of a tree, where there is a cooler temperature and a breeze, making it pleasant for them to remain outside. The person had the physical criteria of feeling hot and the solution of the tree, so they were able to bring those two elements together and adapt them to restore their comfort level. If we were aware that the energy, not the temperature, in our home was hot and sticky, we would adjust it to make it comfortable again. We are, however, unable to sense it, with the result that nothing is changed and we continue to feel uncomfortable without knowing why.

The energy between family members can sometimes overlap if they live in the same dwelling. By sharing the same environmental energy, they will, for obvious reasons, absorb that energy into themselves. To some extent, their interactions with outside influences will modify their energy. Overlapping of energy is common in mothers and children. Stories are told of a mother seeing a vision or hearing a voice at the exact moment when her child is hurt or killed. This happens through the overlap of energy between them. The mother must take precautions, however, to preserve her own personal energy and not allow it to be depleted by any impact on the child's energy. This is done by surrounding herself with a bubble of white light, while still allowing some energy to connect to her child.

The energy I work with during a healing is unlike the energy which flows within a home. I access white light energy from the highest vibrational level of the universe. I also bring this to myself, as soon as I wake up in the morning. The process takes just five minutes, while I allow the white light through my crown chakra to my essence at my center. I also envelope myself, my family and my home in a bubble of this white light for protection. The energy of my body begins each day in an absolute pure state, so it is up to me whether it remains as such, or I allow it to be tainted by my own words or actions or the words or actions of others. The bubble of white light is very resilient, but it is not permanent. I must repeat this process at the start of each day and prior to a client's arrival for a healing consult. As an experiment to ascertain the power of white light, I went for a walk. I passed a yard with a dog which always barks. I enveloped myself in a bubble of white light and focused to block all sight, scent, hearing and sense of me by the dog. It was successful. I passed the dog and it did not bark. When I went past the dog on my return, it still did not bark. I had, in effect, made my energy invisible to it with the cloak of white light, thus, in effect, making myself invisible.

Since everything is energy and the energy of objects can be dismantled so that it loses its solid form, it follows that objects can also be created from energy. If we were to have a thought, it would materialize in our brains as it is energy. It might, therefore, follow that if we were to visualize an object, it could materialize. This probably will not happen directly in front of us. The energy of our visualization would happen in the spiritual realm, be converted to energy and cause the energy of the earthly plane to materialize it. This might sound high-tech, but, when dealing with energy, anything is possible.

As individuals, we are unique and have unique perceptions from the physical level. This results in the same experience being perceived differently. On the earthly plane, a thought uses brain function to be created, then the energy is converted into speech by causing a mouth movement, sending energy through the air to be received into the listener's ears, triggering the brain function of hearing, then understanding. All these steps are necessary so that we can talk to each other. Since our personality and our method of perception factor in, three people could have a totally different understanding of the same statement.

When energy is received from the spiritual realm, it comes directly, clearly and definitively, bringing a distinct message. It still takes some ability to receive the energy of the message, accept it within the soul and then to present it as words. Receiving messages has to be conducted in the soul to avoid any interpretation by the brain processes. Consequently, three different spiritualists would each receive a similar message from the same spiritual energy. In this way, due to its purity, spiritual energy from higher vibrational levels differs from the lower level energy in objects, our homes, workplaces and bodies. Each one of us can, however, choose to bring this higher level energy into our homes and integrate it. If this choice is not made, energy in our body and environment will become stagnant, plugged and thick, translating into many unfavorable issues in our life and health.

5
The soul

During contemplative moments, we might ask why we are on this earth. Is our physical body the only part of us on this earth? When our physical body dies, does that mean the end of our existence? In that particular case, it absolutely would mean this. If there were a part of us which continued to survive after the demise of the physical body, then we could continue to endure. That is indeed the case. The soul is that part through which we continue to prevail.

When a loved one is in the last hours of life, their soul will reconnect with their essence within their body. At death, their soul then leaves the body and travels to the other side. That person's living physical presence is no longer around us. We begin to miss them and feel disconnected from them. After the passage of a little time, when we have found a way to deal with the pain of mourning, we should know that we can still have a connection with them. We can still continue to give love to them and receive love from them. We can even resolve unsettled issues, such as healing the regret of having had an argument the last time we saw each other. The souls, who have passed on, need the resolution, the forgiveness and the renewed love from us so that their soul can continue to evolve where they now are. When we pass on, we have to enable our soul to evolve into its purest form, thereby necessitating unresolved issues on Earth to be reconciled. For many people, the souls of their loved ones can approach them, but since they are not seen, there is no discussion and no resolution to unfinished issues. If the soul and their family members on Earth could come together with a person, such as a medium, then through mediation a resolution to some issues could possibly be achieved. When the soul leaves at the death of the body, it advances to a realm parallel to our earthly one. This parallel realm seeps into my earthly realm so that I am able to read that energy and connect to receive information from the other side.

When someone we love departs this life and we are told that their soul is 'at peace', we are happy. Why? Since peace is positive, their passing must also be something positive. Even though we do not have a full comprehension of what this entails, we have an intrinsic hope that it is a good thing. We are left with memories of the person and items which belonged to them. The items carry their energy. The memories are energy. We carry some of this energy within us, if the relationship was close and, in this way, we feel linked to them. We believe it is the most we can expect to have.

The soul has great significance. It is the way we endure eternally. It is also the catalogue of our learning both on Earth and on the other side. After we pass on, we complete on the other side the unfinished earthly lessons of our life. The soul needs challenges if it is to evolve. We choose experiences and challenges in heaven prior to commencing a life. Before returning to this world, we selected our home country, family, culture and health parameters. This included some challenges, which could be a physical or mental disability, a health issue, abuse, loss or a broken relationship. We then begin living our life, meeting these challenges and advancing our soul. After we die, we must have advanced the soul and managed the obstacles to move into a level of evolvement in heaven. We chose the challenges and so must take responsibility for them, find a way to deal with them and get through them. Each level of evolvement in heaven signifies a precise measure of soul advancement. When we next return, after the end of our next life, we will reconnect with that achieved level and continue to advance from that point.

'On paper', these challenges might look achievable for our soul to deal with and solve, thus enabling it to advance. A familiar analogy of this in our present reality would be to set up an errands list for the day. The list looks feasible, but then we begin to perform the many tasks and discover the huge undertaking which we did not anticipate. Usually, the list is left unfinished and some tasks are partially complete. This is how some of us approach our heavenly list. We sometimes overestimate our ability, since our focus is only to advance and evolve our soul significantly. We are guided and shown how these events would translate on Earth, but sometimes zeal overtakes us. Life then begins and we are handling it from the physical reality of the Earth plane and it is very alarming to us how these challenges are transforming into reality. To surmount them, we need to use all the extensive resources available to us. With support in both realms, everything can be overcome.

During the selection of challenges, perhaps we believe that, if we select one very difficult trial, we need not undertake several lesser challenges, which would equal it. We receive sympathetic counseling in this selection process from spiritual guides. Such was the case for my dear mother. I was born as a triplet, a challenge in itself for my parents in the decade we were born. My elder triplet sister died at three months old in hospital due to a hospital error. With no family support system, no social assistance and needing still to attend to my elder brother, surviving triplet sister and me, this must have been extraordinarily overwhelming for both my parents, especially my mother. Their characters were, thankfully, made of resilience and strength and they pushed through each day. The trauma, which their souls must have held, can only be imagined, but somehow they found a way to struggle through it and adapt. As time passed, they did the work that was necessary for their healing and many years later reached a phase when some balance and happiness came back into their lives, but there would never be a return of complete joy. We, their children, never felt unloved or uncared for. We all remained close all our lives, so they did resolve completely the challenge of creating a loving and supportive family.

Had my mother known the heartbreak, which was to ensue, would she have set up this same challenge in heaven before she began her life as my mother? To learn this answer would provide me with powerful learning. My mother has passed away, so, for this book, I asked the questions and read the resulting energy. I learned that my mother regretted living the brutal reality of losing an infant, especially in such a needless way as a hospital mistake. She would not predetermine such an immense challenge again in life. She would instead consider selecting several lesser challenges. I was stunned to learn that I and my two sisters also had to agree to this event. There is no greater loss than a mother losing a baby, but my sister and I also lost our sister and grew up missing her. It did change my life. I appreciated that my mother had the immense courage to tell us about our sister when we were old enough to understand. My mother's soul and my father's soul were advanced after this, but the cost in life could not be rationalized.

It is difficult to accept the notion that some of the intense sufferings we undergo in life is not the result of random events, but have been predetermined by us. It is disturbing to realize that murder has also been predestined by an order of events beyond a person's control. This is sometimes referred to as fate. The phrase 'in the wrong place, at the wrong time' is sometimes used to describe such an event, where any effort made by the victim to evade a horrifying act is futile. The victim had not predetermined that they would die at the hand of a murderer, but only that their life would end at a predetermined age. From the point of view of the spiritual plane, the age was predetermined, but not the exact circumstances until the sequence of events came into being. This person, who has chosen to live a short life, has also chosen challenges, which are achievable in a short span of time. Upon completion of the challenges, their life will end. We hear of such people being described as having lived a full life for such a young person.

From the point of view of the earthly plane, it seems nonsensical and absurd that a life could end in murder. The ugliness of murder exists in our world. Murder takes victims needlessly, ending their lives and traumatizing their families. This is not the way that freewill was intended to be exerted.

Allowing the freewill of the world leaders has permitted war to occur. The noble notion of people joining the military to defend their country is inspiring, but the act of war and its aftermath of death and devastation is unconscionable. Countless lives are terminated or ruined. Cities with dwellings and hospitals are destroyed. From these ashes, however, the optimistic freewill of people arises and perseveres. Perhaps the only plausible way to accept the reality of war is in the context of our human learning, that we should at all costs avoid acts of aggression in the future. The sacrifice of the honorable soldiers and innocent civilians could be perhaps justified if this lesson could be learned.

Some of the emotions of unresolved trauma we suffered in a past life remain with our soul and can be carried on to the next life. In that current life, basic coping mechanisms are actuated and we might do uncharacteristic things or have certain impulsive emotional needs, which we cannot explain. This is because we are reacting to the emotions carried over in our soul, not the emotions of our present life. The carryover emotions are ever-present and continually affect our life until they are removed, whereby their influence is terminated. These residual emotions could lead to confusion and affect us deeply on the mental level. This would then overflow into our relationships, making it difficult for us to maintain a happy relationship or marriage. Thus past life trauma can perpetuate current trauma and even create future trauma. This might cause some people to turn to alcohol or substance abuse to appease this confusion. When this situation escalates, the feeling of despair might become unbearable and lead to suicide. All this due to the fact that we did not recognize nor understand the source of our emotional confusion. To avoid this, we should identify the energy pieces of our soul, representing the causal events, which fled to the spiritual level during trauma, leaving the issue unresolved. Restoring them within the soul will bring the resolution and will heal the soul. This does not happen on its own. Specific intention must be set to make this happen.

An incomplete soul will impact our life detrimentally on the physical, emotional and mental levels. We might find we repeat the same failing cycles or welcome a person with character flaws into our life, without understanding why. This would then manifest into unfavorable outcomes in our life. Pieces of the soul are not constantly fleeing, causing a depletion of the soul and then a total annihilation. The soul is still absolutely intact, as it is only the energy pieces which fled, but it does require healing. The conclusion that those people, who experience more trauma, have so many missing pieces that they have less of a soul, is not valid. The fact that we live each day, getting through our issues and resolving them, replenishes the energy of our soul, but does not return the missing pieces, as this requires the specific intent of a soul healing.

This is an analogy of the soul losing energy pieces. You are sitting on a bench, looking through a box of old family photographs. A gust of wind takes some of the photographs out of your hand and scatters them. You begin to collect them. You are not sure how many are missing. This upsets you as the photos have importance. Believing you have collected them all, you examine the photos in the box and notice that the photo of your grandparents is missing. Your search is unsuccessful and this saddens you, so you search again the next day. Eventually, you locate it and return it with the other photos. You have retrieved all the photos and you feel happy. While the photos were missing, the people, represented on them were not missing, as it was only the photos which were missing.

Once the process of retrieving the pieces of the soul has begun, the physical, emotional and mental levels will begin to come into balance, reflecting positively in our life. We can begin to move on in life, while still pursuing the resolution of existing issues until we have a complete soul. A complete soul will, however, still encounter challenges, as this is the purpose of life and the reason we are on this Earth.

It is complex to understand the act of committing suicide. A person chose to terminate their life as events had become too unbearable for them to endure, or that their thought processes were scrambled and concluded that this act was the only solution. This act caused the demise of their body, but not of their soul. Their soul is perfect, vital and aspiring to evolve. Their soul continues to exist. It is the premature death from harrowing circumstances that is predetermined, not the act of suicide. Suicide can happen on the Earth plane when the marred circumstances combine to make it feasible. The predetermination of the possibility of suicide is agreed upon by all family members. Suicide leaves a tormenting impact on the family members, but having to deal with it supports their soul evolution. The lesson of suicide is an extremely difficult one to conclude on the other side.

It is not instinctive to us to know how to reach the soul. Most of the healing in our life lies outside of the realm of the physical, so it can never be healed by the brain, from the physical. The issues are in our body, but the solution is at soul level. I have found that people have undergone a major change on the physical level, the body, during their life, but their soul remains untouched, unaltered and unevolved. Consequently, the issues, which they have had all their life, still exist in their soul and still negatively impact their life. If a change is desired, a change needs to happen. The person would have to instigate the change within their soul or seek a person, who can assist them with this.

The two levels of physical and the soul are not separate but are intrinsically linked by energy. One level will impact the other and the energy of the two levels will become intertwined, making it difficult to extract the harmful energy. Trauma in living life affects the soul, creating missing energy pieces. These missing pieces have an influence on how one perceives and reacts to events in life. Consequently, more trauma may result, causing more issues to the soul. A cycle is created. Even though people might have repressed traumatic incidents from their childhood, which are now no longer held by the brain, the soul still has an awareness of this trauma. The soul level should be accessed and the issues dealt with for the cycle to be broken.

If the issues are not managed at soul level, people will consequently be trapped in the same repetitive, unproductive cycles of their life and feel stuck, depressed, unable to advance, which will then manifest as physical health issues. These people then focus on healing the physical, but the issues lie untreated at the soul level and they are not reaching that. Consequently, their issues will keep repeating and will continue to degenerate their body, their life. If this cycle remains unbroken, their past trauma will perpetuate future trauma.

The soul has to be reached, taken to the highest level, where the healing is acquired and the soul then conveys this healing through the essence to the emotional, mental or physical levels. All healing can be done at the soul level, but only a fraction can be done at the physical, the brain level. The details of this process will be described in the next chapter.

When I see a client, I 'read' the energy of their soul, whether this is during the healing, or while speaking with them during a consult. Their soul houses all the information they need in their life. Although the distressing situation of a past life does not exist in the current life, a soul still carries a soul echo of that emotion, adversely affecting the current life. When I read the energy and soul echoes of a person's soul, this brings me the guiding information they need. If people only knew that this helpful information existed to be accessed, they could have all the answers to their life. This information has come to exist in the soul through the learned lessons of past lives, higher level knowledge and answers to prayers from the universe. Their soul also holds their past and present trauma and pain. If the deep resolution could be given to them through Soul Healing, this trauma and pain could be released. The soul spaces would be filled, completing the soul and this trauma would no longer have a detrimental effect on other areas of their life. They would be freed. The issues held in the soul are not to be looked upon as a burden, but as the lessons to be learned, to be unlocked and then released. It is a necessary circumstance so that our soul can constantly evolve.

This next example will illustrate why healing has to happen more in-depth, at the soul level. I worked with a client who was unable to sleep, getting only about two hours of sleep per night. The doctor had prescribed over the past two years a gamut of pills to induce sleep, but with no success to achieve sleep. During a healing, I read that this issue had carried over from a past life when he had been a soldier on sentry duty. Since the enemy was close, he remained on guard and did not sleep for three days. Utter exhaustion eventually overcame him and he fell asleep, leaving the camp and other soldiers vulnerable. The enemy attacked, killing them all. His soul carried immense guilt for the death of his comrades. This carried over into the sleep of his current life. He was unintentionally not allowing himself to fall asleep or be asleep and waking himself up numerous times through the night. The soul echo was the emotion of guilt and inflicted on him the deprivation of sleep in the attempt to atone for his culpability for not staying awake and guarding his camp. This explanation was understood by the client as it was reasonable. He accepted the logic but was still unable to sleep. This is because he had heard the explanation with his brain and the issue still existed in his soul. A soul energy part had fled when the incident happened, creating a space within the soul. Until this part was retrieved, welcomed, received, accepted and the space filled, the problem would not be resolved and sleep would remain elusive. A Soul Healing retrieved the soul part. The client welcomed it and a healing was done for it to be accepted into his soul. This completed his soul regarding this incident. No soul echo for the emotion of guilt now existed. That very night, he slept six hours. For the past five years since the Soul Healing, he has averaged seven hours of sleep per night.

Some people gain weight unintentionally. Usually, this is as a result of deep trauma in their early present life. Girls, boys, women and men, who have been the victims of rape or sexual abuse, usually turn to eating more food as comfort and also subconsciously creating a protective shield around themselves. They have the belief that they are protecting themselves from the horrific memories or from a reoccurrence of the crime. It is the logic of the brain which is providing the solution of creating armor around the body through eating. If this leads to obesity and with the probability of other conditions such as diabetes, the doctor will recommend that the weight should be reduced. They will, however, find that they can reduce calorie intake, but the weight will not shift. They are carrying a protective cocoon, a shield. The underlying issue exists at soul level, but they have a shield of extra weight around the body. We have to look to the soul to release the causal issue, prompting the symptom of the extra body weight to be treated. Healing at the soul is necessary to access the issue, address it, heal it and thus eliminate it.

I have worked with clients who have endured sexual abuse and have cocooned themselves with additional weight. To address and resolve their issue takes several weeks. Each session must be handled with extreme compassion to enable the client to feel worthy and know that they were not responsible for what happened to them. Throughout the healings, after releasing the causal issue within their soul, the person would be literally giving up a part of their body by reducing the weight. As they began to see themselves without the protective cocoon, their self-confidence would be restored and they would no longer feel vulnerable.

During discussions with clients, I have learned that some are dealing with a problem in their life, which they absolutely cannot resolve and typically, this is when they come to my practice. Their issue is locked in their soul and they cannot retrieve it in a dream, during hypnosis or in meditation. If the client were to resolve it themselves, they would have to access it during a journey by connecting with the highest vibrational levels of energy. If the issue is allowed to increase in severity and become disturbing, it could potentially cause energy pieces of the soul to leave. This would lead to further aggravations in their life.

My negative experience at school caused an energy space within my soul, as I was a very young child and lacked the knowledge to limit its impact. My parents were hesitant to take on the school establishment on my behalf, so I was left with the energy echo of a feeling of inferiority. I had no one to turn to and felt alone and abandoned. From one single incident, the emotions of degradation, inferiority and loneliness came to subsist in my soul. At a time when a young person begins to experience life, this was counterintuitive. The likely result of these emotions would be a fear to get on with life or a fear to be alone. This did not happen. Intuitively, although unknowingly, I would bring healing into myself, so my soul did not have the opportunity to store any feelings of inferiority or loneliness. As I grew up, I knew instinctively the questions to ask of the spiritual realm. I did release the negative energy and was healed at the soul level. I felt motivated to take advantage of the opportunities in life; living in a large city, choosing to live in another country and starting a career. I had no issue with being alone and enjoyed living on my own for eight years. I got on with my life and began to see very spectacular events unfold. My life could have been very different, likely unsatisfactory, had I not accomplished my own healing.

After our life ends, we live purely at the soul level on the other side, also known as heaven. This being true, we seldom access that level while on Earth. Such is the conundrum of not being able to access the soul, but needing to access the soul if healing is to happen, so that we can move on to enjoy a fulfilled life. Working on improving ourselves on all the levels of physical, mental, emotional and spiritual progresses our soul. It is much the same as doing exercises or walking for our health; when we do the exercise, we see the results and when we do not exercise, no result will happen.

We are able to hear with our soul. We can hear music and really enjoy it, creating a positive feeling within us. This is when it touches the soul. When I hear ancient Tibetan music, it resonates greatly within me. It brings contentment when it echoes with my soul. The medium of music can touch us, transform us, take us to a place where our mind can be unlocked and we can begin to visualize.

We grow up learning customs and this lies deep within us, operating as our fundamental frame of reference. We consider it a truth in our life. We have, however, two truths. One truth is this fundamental of our life, the basis on which we learn during our early life and is derived from our birth country, our parents and our environment. Other influences later come into play; societal, peers, society, altering those fundamentals and no longer the original basis. If we now have an inaccurate set of fundamentals and our entire life is based on these, then there is very little truth reflecting in our life, just at the crucial stage when we are embarking on our adult life.

The second truth is the fundamental of our soul. This is not altered by societal or peer influences. This is pure truth. The soul is where the truth has to be received. This is where our life can change. Hence, we change our life by bringing truth into our soul, not into our life, then our soul does bring its truth into our life. In this way, we will live our life on a basis of continuously evolving pure truth. Since this happens through the soul, it has to be conducted in the spiritual realm. Usually, this is done during a Soul Healing or a journey. Only through the soul, do we have the capability of reaching and seeing the truth of our life. Truth always exists for us. It is concealed and just needs to be uncovered. The truth of our life can become hidden again when we gravitate back to the comfort and familiarity of the inaccurate set of the fundamentals of our life. This temptation is powerful, as this set of criteria is still a part of us, ingrained in our fibre and enmeshed with the triggers of familiarity.

During Healing consults, I see that people often lie to themselves. This is not intentional since people are not even aware they are doing this. They have illusions, not the same as goals, and they have based these on a flawed set of fundamentals of their life. This creates a mess with the end result that they cannot achieve resolutions to the issues in their life. But now, they are trying to function through all that. Compounding with this is that their life does not reflect truth. The truth lies in the soul, unbeknownst to them that a soul even exists. Their attempt will absolutely not work. Truth is needed to be brought into their life.

Such is the extent of influence that the soul has in our life. It holds our secrets and, much to our surprise, we ourselves do not know the secrets of our own soul. These secrets will remain there until we recover them. When I see a client, I receive the echoes of their soul within my own soul. I will transfer this energy to words so that I can speak to the person in front of me, who might think that I am merely speaking, but I am constantly receiving and transferring energy. Whatever information I receive in my soul, I must give it full respect by sharing it with the client. It is, after all, their information. I do not evaluate, filter or paraphrase the information, but deliver the complete messages. This might be perturbing if I were to hear the word 'alcohol', for example. My instinct would be to re-evaluate what I had received, but I have to trust. Of course, this word was given to me in no other context than alcohol abuse. I then share the word with the client. Since I can read that energy in the person, I broach this subject as gently as I can. I reassure them that I do not judge, but they feel shame that I now know their secret. Healing can take place during the Soul Healing when the causal issue will be addressed. If the person is willing to go through the healings, recovery is guaranteed.

I have found that people are embarrassed that I might learn their secrets through energy reading or discover their secrets during a healing. They worry about possibly disclosing personal and sensitive details during a consult and afraid of what they will have to change in their life. They need not have any fear. I am very respectful of their information and it is kept strictly confidential. This delicate information does not change how I relate to them as a person. I do not judge. Judgement cannot enter when I am processing from my soul the information they share. I bypass my brain, which most likely is eager to express numerous opinions. I do not need nor use opinions; I obtain pure information from the person's soul and deliver guidance through my soul. This is the basis for their healing. Since energy from the highest vibrational levels is at work, the healing is conducted totally at the soul level for the person and there is no opportunity for their brain to corrupt it. I am there to bring them healing. Regrettably, many clients do not return after an initial consult as they were not ready to acknowledge their issues, let alone to change them.

When I read and see an area of pain in a person's energy during a healing, this could emanate from suffering recently experienced, or current suffering, or it is in the person's energy field and is imminent for them. Other signs will corroborate which of these options is applicable, which will be validated during a discussion and suggestions will be given.

Energy readings and modifications create positive results, but each person has the freewill to receive and accept this, or not. People deal with the healing process differently; some think too much with their brain and do not go into a relaxed healing rest; others allow the healing to connect with their spirit and go into a deep rest; some people journey. There is no expected way, nor incorrect way to experience a healing. Whatever the person does during a healing is correct and will achieve beneficial results. Good outcomes will always result for the person, ultimately improving their life.

Imminent future occurrences can be read in our energy field, a meter wide band surrounding our physical body. This is not the aura. Although the aura and energy field overlap around us, they are separate and have distinct functions; the aura is an external manifestation of particular colors of our chakra (red, orange, yellow, green, blue, indigo, violet) depending on which chakra is dominant; the personal energy field brings more critical information to us about our well-being, future health issues and our happiness.

We can bring the occurrences of the energy field closer in or move them away from us. Consider the example of the energy of a virus in our energy field. It has formed, attracted to the weakened and overstressed environment of our physical body. We do not wish to draw it into ourselves, transforming it into physical illness. We would thus look after our body by destressing, increasing our body temperature and having a vitamin fortified diet, making our body no longer an attractive environment for this viral energy. The energy is no longer attracted to the energy in our body and is repelled from our energy field. This can be viewed as a helpful warning from our energy. This type of straightforward concern does not need to be solved at the soul level and can readily be resolved from our energy field to benefit our physical level.

The healthcare system in the western world is huge. There are alternative medicine centers, but they form a very small proportion in the healthcare system. Doctors, hospitals, medical practitioners, medical laboratories are all very busy every day with waiting rooms filled with people with minor to serious ailments. These doctors are all attending to the physical body. If people were more cognizant of the relationship of the physical body to the soul and that the solutions lie in our energy and the soul, they would not have to endure the ailments, the crippling, the pain, the depression and the disorders. This solution would generate a tremendous reduction in the impact on the healthcare system. The funds saved could be used to alleviate hunger and homelessness throughout the world.

One might question whether all health issues can be cured from the soul. Supplementary to health issues being cured, the soul has the ability to prevent the ailments from materializing in the first instance. Much as the healthcare system offers an annual physical checkup and blood tests as a preventative routine and to alert the doctor to potential health issues, so the soul holds the alerts for our health. If we were to access this information and act upon it, health issues would be circumvented in advance.

Hence the soul holds a vast array of data in its library of useful information; trauma from our past lives, trauma from our childhood, present challenges, current health issues and life's challenges which will transform into potential life and health complications. This information lingers, awaiting our resolutions. It is never erased nor distorted. It is whole and pure and in the same form as when it was originally created. It exists in the highest level of energy and can thus maintain its purity and its integrity. Once we access the information, it can be utilized and is then changed or eradicated. The next chapter describes this process.

It can happen that a body, which is healthy, is unexpectedly terminated due to a tragic accident, ending that life. This is out of the control of the present life as it was predetermined by the soul before that person's life began. It is difficult for us to accept that, when it is 'our time' to leave, it is our time. We all decided 'our time' before we began our current life, but our exit time could not, however, be pinpointed to one particular day. This would be determined by whether a series of circumstances has occurred to cause that timing to be activated. Hence we do not know how much time we have in this life. Every person has the expectation, no doubt, that they will live a long life. This might cause them to spawn a lackadaisical attitude to life, that there will be many tomorrows to rebuild their relationship with their children, or to ask for forgiveness from a colleague, or to support a spouse, or to do a good deed. One day, there will not be another tomorrow. We must, therefore, build the bridges or seek the forgiveness or do the good deed today. However awkward it might be, we must communicate and connect.

A person does not have to depart this life for the life of their loved one to change. Our life could alter in a single day if we are given a health crisis to face. For a couple, this would mean the start of a challenging phase of their life if one of them became ill. This might not necessarily happen in their twilight years. Their life and the life of the immediate family would be transformed at the roots. All the plans of traveling when they retired or spending more time with friends when the children graduated from school would be put on hold, with the looming dread that these plans might never materialize. Spending special times together, talking and laughing would also be on hold. Regret is not an emotion we should nurture. We should live with no regrets and seize the opportunity to laugh and communicate today.

The conventional method of communication we have in the physical realm is by using the mouth and words to speak and ears to hear it. Many of us have problems doing this, so to consider the method of spiritual communication, will most likely be out of reach. There are many ways to communicate using energy. This process does not involve words, the mouth or ears and could be used on a person who is unable to communicate in the conventional way.

A person may be alive, but in limbo with living, such as a person in a coma. This person's family still has that person in a live state although normal communication is problematic. They wish for the person to wake up and these channels of communication to be re-opened so that they can say all the things they regret not saying when they were still conscious. They could be granted that chance if the comatose person were to wake up, or they might be left with their regrets if the person were to die never having regained consciousness. The family has no choice but to wait.

It would, however, be possible to speak to the spirit of the comatose person. Their soul and their essence are trapped in their static body, but their spirit and soul are very much alive and vibrant. To receive the energy of their soul, it would require that a person link their soul at the highest vibrational levels of energy and engage with the soul of the comatose person. Energy would be received from the soul of the comatose person and could then be translated into words. This would occur in two directions, so that there would be, in effect, a simulation of communication between the two persons. This would indeed be a miracle for the family.

A person, who is mentally challenged, cannot be shown how to leave their brain to link with the spiritual level. This does not imply that they cannot communicate with spirit, as they have an intrinsic ability to do this naturally. There might be more success in communicating with this person's spirit at the spiritual level rather than by traditional communication on the physical level.

Communication between souls can also happen in another context. A person, who has passed on or is still alive, might reach out to my soul through their soul. This happens in a journey I am experiencing prior to or during a client healing. This soul would thus be connected to the client. The soul does not usually give me their name, as I might know them from previous healings and my brain might access that library of information relating to them and create preconceived impressions for me. The integrity of all information is maintained on the soul level, thereby bypassing my brain. When information has been successfully given to me, then a name might be revealed. All the information presented to me would be delivered to the client, who would have the task to recognize them. These healing messages are shared by the soul through me as an intermediary so that the client might learn a lesson or heal from an issue. If the message is from the soul of a person still alive, it is because that person is unable to communicate their feelings face to face yet still wants the client to know how they feel. It all emanates from the standpoint of love.

When we show courtesy and gentleness to each other, our spirit receives this positive energy and it nourishes our internal energy, our essence and our energy field. These courtesies have no direct healing effect on the soul, but their nurturing energy bathes it in white light. A compliment given to another person nourishes the soul. Through societal exchanges, we are taught to be humble and not to have any grandiose view of our self. Although we seem to have developed an innate reflex to reject compliments, we should be readily accepting them. It creates positive energy. We require gratification. Although we do not perform the good acts merely to have them acknowledged with thanks, it is certainly welcomed. We do the good acts for the validation of our worth as a good soul.

We are connected to certain souls. As an example of this connection; we hear about a person losing a child in an accident and we feel very sad for them, understanding that they must be very distraught. This distress will become part of their life every day and perhaps forever. As time passes our feeling of distress for them would wane, as we would no longer be connected to this incident and loss. If it were our own child or the child of a close family member, however, who had been involved in the accident, the situation would be different indeed and the sorrow would persist. Our spirit deals with a situation in the context of any connection. Our soul is only impacted by a direct connection. Our spirit, not our soul, would have been affected to learn of the family's misfortune of losing a child. We are not connected but are still empathetic. Their soul would have been affected by their loss. Our soul would only be impacted were it to be our child, who was in the accident. Perhaps this is a skillful safety mechanism since we cannot carry the weight of everyone's loses and distresses and suffer the huge effect this would have on our soul. The burden would become unbearable. We did not choose that specific challenge for our life. It is not our burden to carry, but we can still be compassionate.

We need to reach a level of understanding of our soul. The understanding of language is a phenomenon. If a language is heard and the listener has no understanding of that particular language, sounds and jabber are heard with no sense gained, so no communication happens. As soon as a language is heard, which the listener can speak, the brain can process the sense and there is total comprehension, and communication can ensue. Such is the case for the language of the soul, hearing and understanding messages from the other side. We have to train our soul to learn the language so that we can hear and understand what is presented.

Our connection to another person might exist even though the person has always been absent from our life. Such is the case for adopted children and their connection especially to their birth mother, or to their birth father. The connection exists in their soul, so they feel the urge to learn more about the connection with that person, even though it might have lasted only one day. Even though many adopted children had incredible parents who raised them, they are still compelled to seek out their birth parents and understand why the connection was severed. Their soul carries emotions of being unwanted, being given away and left with feelings of worthlessness. They feel the need to reconnect with that person again. When they become adults, some begin to search for their birth parents. Many are successful in achieving a meeting when emotions will be released and hugs will be given. So cathartic is this meeting that it brings healing, activating the soul energy pieces, lost as a result of the separation, to be retrieved and received individually into their souls. It is at such an occasion of intense emotions that soul energy pieces can be retrieved without the need to connect to higher vibrational levels of energy.

With constant perseverance to learn about the soul, an incrementally greater comprehension will result. We must strive to become a soul in the leadership of our own life. We must determine the path we wish our soul to take. Intuition can suffice as the transitional tool to be used until a deeper and true appreciation of our soul is learned.

6
The soul and energy

The soul is the ingenuity of exquisite creation. My path has led me to be focused on the soul for my healing work; to retrieve information through my soul and to bring this information to a person's soul for healing, which will prompt an improvement in their life and health. It is achieved by guiding energy in combinations of various energy types and modalities through my soul. The detailed process of a Soul Healing will be described in a later chapter.

Since freewill has to be respected, I cannot implement the process which radically alters a person's life without their full understanding. I take the time to explain the details so that they comprehend and approve each step we take. A person's freewill will certainly not wish to persist in having pain, thus I can alleviate their physical agony directly and help them avoid future pain. This will provide vital energy to them so that they will feel invigorated to take on life's challenges. I receive the messages to alert them to the issues disrupting their life, but can only guide them into using this information, as they must choose when and how to integrate this into their life. Their issues will be traumatic, even long-forgotten, but will have had or are still having a detrimental impact on their life. The person's awareness of the tools and the secrets held in their spiritual realm is a primary step, but utilizing them diligently and consistently to improve their life will be the demanding task. Results will equal the work dedicated to making them happen. People want good health, or a loving spouse, or a child, or a best friend, or sufficient money, but cannot bring themselves to do the spiritual work to make that happen. Hence they simply continue to long for these things. My work is to help them break out of that cycle. Over a few months, I am by their side helping them navigate the process. I have spent thirty years getting to the point of being able to help people with the techniques of life improvement, so I have done the hard part for them! All that remains for them to do is to listen, accept and practise the tasks. Each person has to complete a unique set of tasks, exclusive to their soul, which I initiate for them. While doing these tasks, they will undeniably see affirmative results. They will also have the tools to meet and overcome any future challenges of life.

Most every human being uses the brain without conscious effort, but not many of us use the soul. Many of us do not know what the soul actually does. The way to discover the soul is to get out of the brain and connect from our essence. With a lot of practice, you can clear your brain and link with elevated vibrational levels of energy. These higher vibrational levels are a separate plane beyond our earthly plane. Meditation does not reach these elevated levels. At this highest level, this is where the secrets are locked away in each person. To reach this, you must visualize a light within you at your center. This can be visualized from the center of yourself, or as if you are looking at yourself. Focus on the sphere of light at your center. This is visualization, not meditation. Any manner of breathing is acceptable, as breath control should not interfere with your focus. You might drift off, which is positive, as this is when the brain has switched off and the essence has taken over to connect with your soul. Your spirit will be elevated to higher vibrational levels, where the soul will link its energy with the energy of your essence. The soul has now taken over to look at your life. This is energy at its most dynamic.

A relaxation will be felt once you have managed to discard that cumbersome physical body. This is the tool you would use to take control over the busy brain, that brain which gives you your next day's schedule while you are trying to fall asleep and wakes you up at 3:00 a.m. to repeat the schedule. With its intense logic, the brain is a block to accessing your true essence within you. It will take some practice to get to the point where you can competently see the light within you and not need to focus with all your might.

The higher vibrational levels of energy are the most pure, the most powerful and the most healing. This is the energy to reach and attain. The soul can link with this energy and heal your life, but this is unachievable for very many people, as they have unevolved souls. Their first step would be to become aware of their soul.

We are solid so we think of ourselves as such. Seeing from the soul defies that. When you free your soul, you are fluid, a new concept for most people. You are able to connect with the higher, the highest vibrational levels of energy. Blending, you create a 'oneness'. You feel 'you', as energy, now merged. This is where you are now able to direct the energy within yourself; move out the energy of a problem, move out the energy of an unhappiness, place the energy to welcome that special person into your life or place the energy to get the desired job. You can visualize exactly what you want in your life. Be precise in the wording of your wishes; a man may wish for a special woman to come into his life and find that a woman, who is collecting money for abused children, might knock on his door! So, his wish was answered, but most likely not in the manner he had hoped.

Since it is quite challenging to get to a stage of soul awareness and evolvement, and a lengthy process to perfect (I spent seventeen years to get to this point), I created *Soul Oneness Power©*. During my own journeys in my early life, I have been seeing images and colors. Over three years, I compiled these unique images and colors and put this knowledge into a book, *Your Empowering Life Healing Journey*, so that other people might benefit from also being able to use this tool. The combined images and colors in the book are like a fast track to achieve the connection of the soul and highest vibrational levels of energy, but some diligence is still required, as, after all, it is Healing Energy, not magic! When colors are dynamic, they make everything around us magnificent and fill us with positive emotions. This is also true of the energy within us. We all have the intuition for this. Use the images and colors to help you retrieve the pure energy. Allow it to flow through you, changing your view, transforming your life. You need to learn to reach the highest vibrational levels of energy and bring these vibrant colors within you and keep them brilliant. Then everything within you and in your space will have this radiance and enable you to attain your optimum in life.

Use the tool of belief and trust to prepare a welcoming energy within yourself. Trust what you see and do not let anything discourage you. Then the arriving energy will bond with this energy of trust, empower your essence and connect with your soul. It is all about getting to know your soul, bringing this power within yourself, so that you are at one with your soul. You need to become whole in order to empower yourself, empower your life. Then nothing is impossible for you.

Balance in the physical body, moderation in our life and having priorities are advocated. Our physical body should contain the appropriate balance of elements. Moderation should be exerted with alcohol consumption, pharmaceutical drug intake, eating unhealthy foods and being sedentary. Priority should be given to the achievement of personal health, creating a family unity and enjoying the journey of life. It is all such a delicate balance, that one inadvertent negative change could trigger the first domino to topple and cascade through several more, impacting other areas of our health and life. To maintain the delicate balance of our body, the energy in our home, the happiness in our life and our accomplishments requires constant monitoring and minor adjustments to energy on a daily basis. This enables the energy in our body and home to be organized and form a strong block to the intrusion of potentially adverse energy. Major imbalances, within us physically and within the energy around us, can cause health issues and potentially cancer.

Physiologically, we have twenty-three pairs of chromosomes, making up our DNA, which is totally unique for each individual. So it is with the energy within us. This explains why one energy tool might work for one person and not work so well for another person. The energy tool would have to be modified so that it would work perfectly for each person. It is a learning process. Once achieved, however, it will work flawlessly every time.

Energy and heat have a connection. In Reiki Healing, energy is transmitted to the healer as Reiki energy and becomes heat. This heat energy is then transferred without contact to the recipient through the healer's hands to initiate healing. This healing heat is energy existing at a higher vibration than the earthly plane. The band of energy in the human energy field immediately around the body is the etheric body or etherbody or aura. It is a very low-level band of energy. The healing heat links with the recipient's etheric body and results in their mind sensing energy beyond the body, thus actuating their spiritual level. This combination is limited to accessing only the middle or lower vibrational levels, so no Soul Healing can be performed simultaneously, as this requires access to the highest vibrational levels of energy.

Sound can also connect with our etheric body to become audible to us. We might on occasion hear a high-pitched whistling in our ears. As we become aware that we are hearing it, it will quickly fade away. This sound originates from a higher vibrational level and combines with our energy field to generate a resonance. We should determine what our thoughts were at the time we heard that sound and while our energy was connecting to a higher level, as the opportunity of hearing messages was being presented to us.

Sleep and rest is a regenerative phase for our body. This is the optimal time to enable our spiritual essence to be dominant. This has the dual purpose of preventing our brain from taking control and getting us up out of bed at 2:00 a.m. struggling to sleep, as well as to connect us with the spiritual level. The brain should be taking instruction, not giving it. It is no coincidence that the crown chakra is located above the brain, so we must give the focus to the crown chakra. Before bed, we should allow the pure white light to enter our body through the crown chakra to drift through and push out any detrimental energy, thus clearing our energy. To put us into that calm, restful state, we should visualize the water in a stream or calm ocean waves. The white light and the water will create the ideal energy for our essence to become dominant and avoid the overbearing domination of the brain. Any interruption of schedules being thrust before us by the brain will be invalidated. Initially, visualization of water will be necessary to relax us, but, as we become more accomplished and are able to determine that the essence is in control, we will be able to bypass visualization and simply enable our spiritual essence directly.

Those people, who cannot sleep, value it and miss its benefits. When someone is sleeping and we walk into that room, we do not speak in a loud voice, but we whisper. This is done because we respect sleep. We do not want the person to be suddenly awakened and be startled. We also do not want to abbreviate the restorative effects sleep is giving them. We allow them to continue receiving the gift of sleep. Alternatively, if we intended to wake them up, we would have to speak utilizing a balance of a volume level between not too loud and startling, but sufficient to be heard in the plane where their mind is, in order to draw them from there.

Getting sleep is rudimentary. Getting restful sleep is more challenging. Getting regenerative sleep is the desired result but is elusive for many people. This is usually because the causal reason for sleep prevention lies at the soul level. The issue to impede sleep happened in a past life or in our childhood. The reason, and thus the solution to better sleep, lies within our soul. A Soul Healing would recover the causal issue and remedy the problem of limited sleep.

As soon as I awake in the morning in my bed, I go through a routine to accept pure white light within me and around me. This enables me to start each day with one hundred percent pure energy to give my day and my life the very best prospect, so that I can be healthy, feel happy and accomplish goals. For this process, I use my mind, not my brain. As this is very relaxing, I sometimes begin to drift into sleep again and my mind wanders away from the process of receiving this energy and is attracted to higher levels, where I can hear messages or see images. My consciousness realizes this is happening, so I pull myself out of this and refocus on the process of receiving pure energy. Sometimes, I begin this cycle two or three times, so alluring is the relaxation.

A parallel for this type of mind drifting can be drawn to Alzheimer's disease, where the mind wanders into another level where it is not focusing on the task at hand. I am, however, able to redirect my mind to concentration, so it begs the question of whether it would be possible for an Alzheimer's patient to be able to refocus their thoughts between the different levels. Once the time comes that the person with Alzheimer's is unable to think habitually for themselves, this does not mean that they are not still whole at their spiritual level with a perfect soul. All their thoughts are still intact at the spiritual level. The key would be to engage with them at this functioning level. It would entail the application of the same procedure as for the comatose person, whereby communication between the souls is established at the highest vibrational levels of energy and energy is used to interconnect. It would be intriguing to hear what thoughts they share about their condition.

Although the body is alive and the person is somewhat mobile, the brain's functions are substantially obstructed by neurodegenerative processes. With the passage of time and if the degeneration continues, this person's cognitive ability of basic systems will begin to fade. Only a shell of the body will remain until the brain is unable to coordinate the functions of vital organs. Throughout all this decline, the spiritual level and soul will remain perfectly intact. Eventually, the person will pass away. It is very traumatic for family members to witness this deterioration. Equally traumatic would be the realization of the missed opportunities to communicate at the spiritual level with the person at the end of their life.

When a medium connects with a person, who passed from Alzheimer's, they will be given the message that the person heard everything the family said to them but were unable to communicate on the physical level. The complete ability of communication, therefore, was still present, existing at the spiritual, not the physical level.

Similar to the Feng Shui 'Bagua Map', which is symbolically overlaid in a house to identify the various zones of the house, representing the respective elements of our life, the body also has a type of Bagua Map. The center, the health zone, is the spiritual zone of the soul and the physical zone of the kidneys. Metaphysically, the kidneys are the center of life, so it is imperative to keep the kidneys strong for our overall physical health. On the spiritual level, the soul is the nucleus and foundation of life and its energy should be kept in wellbeing.

There is a relationship between energy and time in the form of a component of momentum. We are familiar with the concept of time on the earthly plane. We might feel that our lives are ruled by time, as this is the only way to bring several people together at a certain place at a certain time. Time in the universe is not like time on the Earth plane. There is no such thing as time per se in the spiritual realm. Our physical self functions within the parameters of time while on the Earth, while the soul functions in this timeless sphere of the spiritual realm. The soul records traumatic incidents or memorable events and can recall an incident as if it were yesterday, when in fact it took place twenty years ago. The children of the same family can remember the same past incident differently since it has been imprinted with their own perception and rewritten by the passage of time. One child might even not recall it at all, even though they both experienced it. They have accessed the recollection of the incident from the memory bank of their brains and, since they are individuals, it has been catalogued differently for each of them. Were they to access this incident from the information in their soul, the experience of the incident would be exactly as it happened and identical for both siblings.

The soul's cataloguing system is unique and uncontaminated with an opinion. The soul, not being linked to time, always functions in the present, the now. An analogy of the soul's cataloguing system would be a library, which we could visit. We could select a book, which had been written thirty years prior, but the integrity of the words has totally been maintained, so that we are able to read that information exactly as it had been written, in the now. Important or traumatic events are registered by the soul exactly as they happened and with the accurate, relevant emotion that was created. The soul thus solves a current problem, which had been produced from a past traumatic incident, in the now. This is helpful during a Soul Healing when this untainted information can be accessed and delivered to a client for discussion. It is amazing to witness the startled expressions to the information in this pure form. They will experience the situation as if for the first time, although not the traumatic emotion associated with it, unlocking many truths and gaining a profound understanding and healing. If this information were to relate to a trauma, release could then happen and the person would finally be free of this burden.

The soul catalogues the past, solves in the present, but cannot see into the future. It can, however, influence the outcome of future events by resolving issues of the past, thereby granting the person an upgraded energy to apply to their life. Thus there is no need for the soul to have foresight. It needs only to operate in the now. This is also the way we should be living our life; to enjoy our life and be in the now and not to constantly believe tomorrow will bring us improvements or solve our problems. This does not preclude having future events to look forward to, but we must live in the now while these future events come into the present. We can work on realizing future objectives by working with our soul on resolutions in the present.

If you are new to exploring how to connect with the spiritual realm to bring healing and improvements into your life, you have the option of receiving a Soul Healing, but there is also much you can do on your own for yourself. The following are some of the available tools; white light brought through the crown chakra into the center of your body and around you will serve to dispel any stagnant energy blocking you from achieving good results; by using the tool of white light each morning, this would present you with the energy and information to handle the events your day brings; white light introduced through the crown chakra to form a sphere at your center and connect your essence with your soul; introducing *Soul Oneness Power©* into your life would give you the ability to connect with the highest vibrational levels of energy and an in-depth understanding of your life, which will make it feasible for you to begin changing your life; as you fall asleep and are in the in-between plane between sleep and awake, within the alpha and theta planes, this would vitalize the mind to take control over the brain and connect you with the spiritual realm.

The medium of water can be used to conduct sounds. Water from a flowing tap can conduct sounds through the energy of the water, and words could be distinguished. This medium can thus be utilized as a breakthrough point for you to access the spiritual realm. Once that connection is achieved, the use of water would no longer be required. Meditation and journeying would then be effective in facilitating further connections. Water also possesses the energy of extraordinary healing qualities. When we visualize water, the vision and sound are soothing, arresting any anxieties and allowing access to higher energy levels. This can be accomplished through a meditation involving being near water or floating on water.

These tools that I have described use different forms of energy. I personally use them in my life and in my healing work. From years of practice, I have honed them to be more effective, be acquired more quickly and become more personalized to my specific needs, but the common basis of white light and higher vibrational levels of energy is always present. I have many blessings in my life and I thank God for every one of them. I have happiness but still welcome the challenges in my life, as I accept that my soul has to evolve through encountering them but that I do have the resilience to deal with all the ordeals. I need my life to have a forward moving momentum, so that I can develop as a person, but more significantly, so that my soul will evolve.

7
The soul and guidance in life

This is a poignant story. It expresses an event in life, which my elder brother had to endure. It was a time of learning for both of us; he learned about life and I saw all my learning and all my gifts come together at one time so that I could be there for him.

A few years ago, I felt a distinct urge that my brother or sister was going through a serious health issue. They both lived in one country and I lived in a country far away from them. I asked my sister, who reassured me that she was in good health. I asked her about my brother's health and she informed me that he had not mentioned his health. The urging would not leave me. I asked my brother directly and, after two denials, he admitted that he had just received the diagnosis of colon cancer.

Being far away made it very challenging to help him. Immediately, my sister began looking after him, as he lived on his own. We experienced every moment of every appointment and the surgery with him. I did several remote healings a day to keep him peaceful. He was a tall, handsome man with a sartorial style and appeared much younger looking than his fifty-eight years. To see him losing weight and struggling to competently look after his home and himself was distressing. There was a point when he seemed to resign himself that there was no return from this. My sister and I were relentless, however, fighting with everything at our disposal.

I had asked the spiritual realm for a special place to be created where my brother, sister and I could go. At night, I found myself drifting upwards to arrive at a beautiful building. As I entered, I was led to a room filled with very tall windows with no glass and white light streaming in. This light bathed me in a pleasant warmth and brought peace into my heart. I saw three beds. This sanctuary was where the three of us would take our rest and how we spent very many nights. It was a most incredible night's rest. This room was created for the purpose to ease his pain, for us to be together and to bring peace into our hearts.

My sister came to visit me after my brother's surgery. We reassured each other that it could not possibly be the end of his life. Not him. He had finally found a balance in his life and was moving forward. All we could do was to be there for him, help him in any way we could, get him through this, pray and send healing.

The hospital missed calling him to set up a chemotherapy session. They apologized and called it "falling through the cracks", and set up another appointment. He took this as a sign, as he had had major issues with nausea after chemotherapy. He later cancelled the appointment and got on with his life.

Three months later, his condition deteriorated and he went into hospital. The doctor had used the word 'terminal' to him when describing which treatment was available. The cancer had metastasized to his liver so surgery was no longer an option. This news came as no surprise to my brother. He felt he had received confirmation for what he already knew. For my sister and me, it shot a deep pain through our hearts.

My sister visited him every day, taking him outside into sunshine in a wheelchair. I phoned her every day and we talked only about him. I sent remote healing daily to ease any pain, so he did not need morphine, much to the doctors' amazement. I spent many hours during that time, praying and pleading with God not to take him. One night, I had a dream, where I was pleading and I was told that it is my brother's wish and cannot be changed. I was heartbroken. Two days later, he passed away with my sister at his side. My soul was with them. I miss the unconditional love held in the special room we shared. I have not returned to the room, as its purpose was completed. It had been created for us, for this one extraordinary occasion.

Although this happened five years ago, the echoes of the events persist in visiting me every few weeks. It is an enigma to me. He was supposed to have a happy life. It took him a long time to get his life on track after his university studies and the first jobs. We, three siblings, were growing closer and visiting each other more often over the past ten years, exactly as our father had asked us to do, to be the support for each other. My brother was happy for the last ten years of his life. He had gone through the norms of social expectations: school, university, career and finally reached an equilibrium where he had a good career, home, his beloved tango dancing and time to do his research into numbers. Just as he was finding this balance, it all ended. He now knows why. I am, however, still left with the enigma.

I had known him on the physical level and could visit him, talk with him and give him hugs. That had now ended. I had to adjust to knowing him in a special way, on the spiritual level. Therefore, I did not lose him and I still have him, but in a changed way. I have had numerous spiritual conversations with him. I now know the universal reason and explanation for his departure, but my compulsion was to constantly relate it to life on the Earth plane, causing it to distort, recreating the enigma. The loss, the premature end of his life, the longing to spend more time with him would all be restored due to my fragile humanness. To avoid this, I found I had to keep the explanation within the realm, to which it belonged, the spiritual realm.

Dealing with my brother's health ordeal in life was a watershed for my healing work advancement. This was the time when I used all my knowledge and gifts to work concurrently. I am aware that this event happened in his life to become a phase of learning for both of us. I do not have the definitive answer whether he had predetermined to go through the cancer, not only for himself, but also selflessly for me so that I could learn and evolve my work. I must thank him when we see each other again.

Having to go through this tribulation, brought answers to some of my long-standing questions. I had more understanding of a person's choices in life. Cancer does not automatically signify the end of a person's life. People do get through cancer and continue to live long, fulfilled lives. My brother chose to exert his freewill to follow his path to the end of his life and for his soul to begin its existence in the afterlife. My many desperate attempts to keep him here could not override his freewill to depart. I had been told this explicitly from the universe and I understood, but somehow I could not relinquish the hope of keeping him here. My emotion of selfishness fed this notion. I was seeking the easier solution for myself and was being self-centered. He wanted to fulfill what he had predetermined about his life, consequently choosing the opposite of what I wanted. It was very clear; it is his life; it is his choice. I did not consider nor respect the power of freewill until after he died. It was the most extraordinary lesson I have ever learned in my life. I am, however, comforted by the fact that we three siblings had been there for each other, day and night and had shared a most extraordinarily wonderful place.

Even if a solution exists for a person to survive cancer, they can still use freewill and choose to leave their life early in the diagnosis. The challenge of an illness would have been predetermined before their life started. It would also have been predetermined by their entire immediate family. After the challenge had presented itself in their life, they could exert control and choose to exit sooner. This choice would be made to reduce the trauma their illness was inflicting on their family. The person has autonomy within the parameters of the predetermined event over the direction their life will take. Their illness would be a learning experience for the family, during which they would gain a deeper appreciation of life and evolve their souls. Essentially, the cancer patient would be sacrificing themselves for their family. Clarification is needed here to separate this act from that of suicide. The cancer patient did not take their own life by making a choice to exit sooner.

A person has freewill and their energy cannot be accessed by another without their express permission. A person, who understands energy, could technically access and control the energy of another person and have the potential to control that person, which would not serve that person well. This is absolutely not permitted and therefore not possible.

Even the soul of a person has the freewill to decide whether to cross over to the other side or remain attached to the life which had just ended. This is usually the outcome of a tragic event which caused the demise of the body, such as an airplane accident or the sinking of a ship. People have many tales of seeing spirits in human form wandering the decks of old ships, in the area of a sunken ship or onboard an airplane with parts from an aircraft involved in a tragic accident. It is not the airplane or ship which has a spirit, but the trapped souls attached to it. The attached soul believes it is protecting others from this same demise. This is their choice. They have chosen not to begin another life and have made this existence their destiny, as it has a critical significant purpose for their soul. A soul makes this choice only in extreme circumstances.

This story is a powerful example of freewill on a personal level. I met with my very good friend. I will call her Jill. She was a private teacher. She knew that my work was healing and allowed me to read her energy while she taught her student. I found myself telling her to go and see a doctor as there was a problem with her liver and kidney. She told me her physical was coming up and she would ask the doctor. After the physical, she informed me that the doctor had said her health was good. But what I was seeing was persistent and the same scenario between Jill and myself repeated two more times over the next weeks. I received a phone call after Christmas 2013 from a mutual friend. He told me that Jill had passed away in hospital on Christmas Day from liver and kidney failure.

She was forty-five years old. I was devastated and helpless at the same time. I felt helpless, as I had had to respect her freewill to choose. Despite her denials, I had, however, trusted what I had seen and tried repeatedly to have her realize she needed to seek medical help.

I spent many hours getting to an understanding of these events. Jill was a lovely and thoughtful person. Despite this, the elements in her life were challenging: she was in a loveless marriage with a husband who gambled; she looked after his adult son when he visited, whereas his father ignored him; the owners of the space she rented for her teaching were very spiteful to her; her elderly parents were demanding, still treating her like a child to do things for them at short notice. She felt herself being emptied by all these demands.

In the balance of her life, the scale tipped very much to the side of deep unhappiness. She tried constantly to make it better, to see the positive, but it was to no avail. When she received the diagnosis of a liver and kidney issue, she went into hospital. Jill did not disclose to me the true reason for her hospitalization. Although she found it difficult to tell me lies, she did so to protect her decision. She told me that the hospital tests proved inconclusive and that she had a minor bacterial infection, which would clear up. She denied her true condition to me to the end, so that I would not take action to get her help, and so she could proceed with leaving all the trappings of her miserable life. She allowed me to send remote healing, but she was not receptive to it and largely blocked it. After her death, our friend confessed to me that she had told him that I was relentless in encouraging her to get medical help and that what I told her I was seeing was "scary correct". She told him that it broke her heart to lie to me as I was desperately trying to help her. She confided to him that her depression prevented her from seeing value in her perceived miserable life and seeking medical attention, as there was no purpose to continue living.

I had spent numerous late night hours on the telephone with Jill, listening to the latest debacle of her husband or parents and consoling her. As I looked back at these phone calls, I saw how often she had talked about heaven and how beautiful it must be. I put this down to her being spiritual and tried to redirect her focus to this life. This was the innermost plea of her freewill. Whether she was aware of this or not, she was telling me that she wanted to be in heaven. My brain did not receive this message loud and clear. Had she given me the opportunity to do a Soul Healing, my soul would have received that message clearly. For this reason, she never had any intention of allowing me to do a healing, as I would have been even more "scary correct".

I learned from my friend's experience that freewill is mighty. No amount of persuasion or interference will derail a life from its intended course. It is between that person and their God. My compassion will still propel me to help people as ardently as I can, even if I am told that they have chosen a path to finality. I will reluctantly have to accept this and respectfully not attempt to change it.

We should live within the understanding of the relationship between this life and the after-life. If we do or say something disparaging to a person today in order to feel satisfaction at the time and we were to review our feelings about this, we would probably regret having said or done it. This is how we will view our actions and words of this life from the after-life. We will have more forgiveness and kindness in the after-life, putting aside small aggravations, which are too inconsequential to even merit dealing with. Perhaps this lesson should be learned now, while on this earth, in this life. When we pass on and reach the other side, we should not have to face all the minor irritations we could have avoided in life. It is worthier to live now with no remorse on this earthly plane.

In the after-life, our soul concludes the incomplete lessons from our life on Earth and also continues to learn new lessons, so it can further evolve. If we thought that eternal life constituted eating grapes lazily with our bare toes dipping in cool, fresh water, then dream on! Our work continues, so it is better to learn the lessons during our earthly life.

We have kindness and sometimes find ourselves in a situation, where we are unsure about how to use this quality effectively. A wife, caring for her sick husband, might end up carrying him spiritually in the belief that she is caring for him until she physically develops back pain. The consequential backache is a psychosomatic result of her emotional state due to the energy exchange between them. He needs her help to get through his day. She cannot release the backache by releasing him, as she feels she would be abandoning him. Constantly attending to his needs equates to her permitting the continued pain of her backache. The cycle will thus perpetuate.

The good deed of caring for her sick husband had resulted in causing the wife trauma rather than joy. Her soul holds this lesson for her and she must strive to access this, accept it and release it. The acceptance would give her the understanding of the lesson of finding the balance between caring for her husband without absorbing his issues. She would then be able to release all emotions of guilt. The emotion of her abandoning her husband would no longer exist. The backache would be immediately removed. She would be able to look after him without being caught up in the energy of his illness. There would no longer be the need for her to carry him spiritually.

Every person can do self-healing. They need to identify the disagreeable element occurring in their life, focus on it and address it through the soul by using the tools of the images and colors or white light. It will not be instant, although a noticeable improvement will be detected right away. With the consistent use of the self-help tools described in this book, definite progress will be made.

If one single unhappy element in a person's life can be identified, then self-healing is straightforward. People invariably need healing, however, on several levels, or on all levels. Some of these issues are uncomplicated and some are enmeshed throughout all the levels so that they must be individually identified and healed level by level. In the case of issues which are intertwined, it is advisable to seek the counsel of a healer for this complex process, so that the best opportunity is given to the client to welcome, receive and accept the changes.

It is advisable that, after undergoing many consecutive in-depth healings, that the person amend their way of life. We choose what we eat. In the same manner, we should choose which actions we take, which words we speak or which ideas we accept. Being selective, we can prevent energy, which does not serve us well, from invading us and creating plugs, resulting in our being depleted of empowering energy. Since this negative cycle is deeply intrusive and spirals within us, it often leads to depression. Although the brain might be medically treated in this instance, it is the energy within us, which should be evaluated and treated. By not targeting our inner energy, this results in many people being doomed to live with this condition of depression their entire lives.

Annoyances bother us. We become anxious about many situations and this engulfs us totally. If the energy from this anxiety is not cleared, it may lead to an illness. If we are diagnosed with a disease, those bothersome things instantaneously do not seem so significant relative to the new circumstance of our challenging health. Our health now becomes our focus. Perhaps for some people, they predetermined that should they not be respecting and living life, then a disease should happen to put this into perspective. This would be a brutal lesson for a person to be subjected to. Those irritating things should be justifiably handled with minimal attention and be released. In this way, a disease will not need to manifest to train a person in appreciating life.

A negative emotion, created by the brain, manifests itself in our body's cells. This can transform into fear. Fear is a block to accessing our soul and a block to living a fulfilled life. It is essential that we release the fear. Sometimes this basis of fear creates the foundation for cancer cells to develop. If we live our life with no fear, cancer has no environment to flourish. Illnesses are representative of our fears in life, for example, being afraid to go outside, being afraid of people, being afraid to start a new venture. The resulting illnesses are cancer, multiple sclerosis, asthma or emphysema. Cancer can be blocked by allaying fears so that the brain waves can enter a level, where there is no hospitable environment for fear. Heal the situation, thus heal your body and your life.

To have a total comprehension of fear, we must deal with fear. It resides deep within us, so is not readily accessible to be identified and extracted. We must use a severe approach. We must first accept that it exists in us but is not part of us, and therefore we are not losing a physical part of ourselves, like losing an arm or leg. We then confront fear, recognizing its origin, and eradicate it, by understanding that we can bravely face the causal issue. Fear cannot be allowed to exist in us, as the condition will only spiral into an increasingly dreadful series of events. It will certainly not disappear of its own accord, so action must be taken. It is not a coincidence that when the second and third letters of the word 'scared' are switched, the word becomes 'sacred'. There is a link. Rather than being scared to live life, live with a sacred soul to bring you the happy and fulfilled life you deserve.

People often ask, "Why do bad things happen to good people?" The events, which happen in people's lives, are not 'good' or 'bad', but merely circumstances that we are to live through, deal with, learn from and advance from. The emotions we feel are part of this learning, but the emotions must not override how we deal with the event. If we accept that we have predestined these events, brutal as their translation on the Earth plane might sometimes be, we might comprehend it more willingly. This does not imply that we must always develop positive emotions about the event. Having true emotions and feelings are the crucial criteria of the learning. If we must grieve, then we must go through the stages of grief, feel the sadness and the hurt. We will then come through the experience a transformed person.

As parents, we feel we must always be the parent, wanting our child to go through experiences under our supervision to help them acquire the tools to be successful in life. Sometimes we need to be the child, to be the one to be looked after, guided and taught. God looks after us in a similar way to a parent looking after their child. We can be both a parent and a child. Throughout our entire life, we have to go through certain events to learn, even though they might be challenging. These experiences are not intended to punish us. We will advance through dealing with them. As an analogy: if a parent gives a child money for everything they want, the child will not learn the value of working for it, nor the value of money. Similarly, we have to expand our abilities in order to reach everything we need. God does, however, continue to help us throughout the challenges. We need to be willing to continuously learn throughout our entire life. The learning should never end.

We have choices. Our life is a progression of the choices we make. When we arrive at a fork in the road of our life, we might steer ourselves or we might be steered by another person. If we follow the road chosen by another person, we are still making a choice. This is a common situation in a marriage or cohabiting relationship, where one dominating partner makes the decisions for both parties. If both people are satisfied with this and the direction their life is heading, then it is acceptable. If one of the partners, however, unilaterally makes the decisions with no regard to the impact on the spouse's life, then this is objectionable. The parties need to find a balance where separate choices can be made but still advance both lives constructively and, most certainly, the lesson of compromise will be learned by both parties.

As we grow up, some choices we would like to make, are closed off to us, legally or by our parents, with the intent that other people are protecting the vulnerable young person. Although this is a choice in one person's life, made by another person, it is done with the best intention. The young person is being protected from the option of doing a cruel act, while they learn about right from wrong. Every person in the world has basically the same concept of right and wrong, good and bad. Cultures may vary slightly in their understanding or implementation of these words, but, intrinsically, we come from the same standpoint. This is not a coincidence. We share this intrinsic appreciation with each other. In this way, we can understand the feelings or reaction of a person at our first meeting with them.

When I read energy, I trust and understand the energy I am seeing. I am being shown it in terms of something I will recognize. I will see a symbolically black area in a particular location within the body, representing an internal organ needing attention. I will see green sludge in areas where there are plugs of energy, causing other energy to stagnate and no longer be able to nourish the body. I will see ropes with huge knots where the person is bound to an issue from their past or present. This damaging energy will manifest in a person as breathing problems, headaches, back pain, depression or feelings of anxiety. These symptoms become clues to what is needed to be fixed in their lives so that these health issues can be resolved throughout their body.

People look upon the words 'healing' and 'cure' as interchangeable. This is not the case. Healing would have to happen initially to remove the origin of what is causing a person's body to be sick or making them unhappy. Only when the causal issue has been healed is the person able to move toward regaining full health or allowing happiness into their life. Since the healing can remove the deep trauma, which might have caused cancer, there would be no foundation for the cancer to exist. By virtue of the cancer's non-existence, the end result would be a cure for cancer, although it would be achieved through the healing of traumatic issues in a life. Healing operates on the spiritual level and a cure operates on the physical level, but the two levels work in tandem to facilitate the positive end result. I learned from the spiritual realm that healing, which brings about the eradication of cancer in a body, is called a 'solution' to cancer.

When a client is sitting in front of me, I speak to the consciousness of that person. Their brain processes the information, determining whether to file it away as they have understood it or to discard it. The brain is the sentry to our thoughts and can sometimes be very controlling. Any thoughts with an infinitesimal inkling of non-reality are usually not allowed past the sentry. To bypass this blocking mechanism, I bring a peaceful healing energy initially, which relaxes people, so that I am able to successfully reach and read the energy of their spirit directly. It is an eternal dichotomy of brain versus spirit. We are forced to give attention to the brain, but it is the soul, which needs the healing. For this reason, my work operates exclusively on the soul and spiritual levels.

By virtue of coming to me to receive healing, a person is giving me permission to read their energy. Despite this, nothing is done to a person. It is always done for a person with their full knowledge and consent. Freewill is still readily available to them. Spirit cannot get into our brain without our approval. We can, however, choose to have our mind meet spirit at the spiritual realm. This meeting place for the two realms to unite is at a high vibrational energy level. During a healing, a person's essence is guided from the Earth plane to the highest vibrational levels of energy, where it will reconnect with their soul. Only positive emotions will be felt. Unencumbered like this, the soul can evaluate events and meaningful emotions will result. While this process is occurring, I read the messages of this energy and transfer it into my soul to deliver to the person after the healing. After the healing process, the person shares their experience with me and I share my reading with them. Huge progress is made during this time. It is a time of enlightenment for a person.

A person would come to me, not because they are content with their life, but because there are issues and great sadness. They wish their issues to be resolved and that they can be really happy in life. All our endeavors in life are all about our being happy. So why do so many of us not attain this? This is truly an enigma. We genuinely believe we are trying and working hard at being happy. Some people strive a little toward happiness and some do nothing at all and hope that it will just happen for them. Sometimes, we put this burden on the shoulders of another person to make happiness happen for us. We might decide to wait for a sufficient span of free time to begin ardently working at attaining happiness. We believe that time will free up, having finished all those repetitive chores of life and then we will do something about seizing that elusive happiness. This is not a constructive approach, as that free time, of course, will never come. We must live today and focus on putting the elements of happiness into today. Waiting for free time will perpetuate the procrastination. If it is worth having, it is worth working for. When your life is not working for you, then work it, empower it, guide it. We should endeavor to have the best life we can as, all too soon, it is over and we begin our existence in heaven.

Happiness has a broad spectrum of meaning. One popular definition of happiness is that a person has amassed a great deal of wealth and can now simply play and have enjoyment. Many people might leap at the chance of this lightweight fulfillment, but it sustains an unevolved soul if only playing and having enjoyment fill all the time in their life. Some people with great wealth should be commended, as they have found a balance between having the wealth and using it for philanthropic enterprises, thus evolving their soul with the good deed. We do need sufficient finances for the basic necessities of life and therefore not have the worry of being in need of money for the rent or groceries. With the monetary issue under control, a person would then have the inclination to seek avenues to bring happiness. Simple pleasures could bring the greatest happiness. You could find happiness in helping a child learn to read, in doing an errand for an elderly person, spending time playing outside with your children or enjoying an outing with your significant person. The energy created will bring the happiness, which will produce a greater inclination to do more positive actions, thus generating more happiness and so the cycle will continue. Happiness empowers more happiness. We should do this now, for we never know when our final day will be.

A person, in the final moments of life, having completed their living, will embark on reconciling their soul with the realm beyond. Although we refer to them as a dying person, it is only the body that is dying, not the soul. The person might see the spirit of their departed loved ones, who have come to support the departing person. Even if this might be happening while their living relatives are present, the spirits of the loved ones can only be seen by the departing person. Whether the person has been counselled not to speak of what they are witnessing, they do not tell the living relatives what is happening around them. At the end of life, the person passes several times between the spiritual realm and Earth plane. When they return to the conscious realm, they do not return with any information, or, if they do, they do not disclose it. It is similar to waking up from a dream, when you recall snippets or, more often, you cannot recall the dream at all.

Some people have experienced what is now termed a 'near death experience', where they saw the white light of the spiritual realm and relatives who have passed on. They believed that they had visited heaven. They came back to the Earth plane from this place and were able to recount details of their experience. It is not a miscalculation on heaven's part that this occurred. It is intentional for that particular person to have been given this experience to share with others. Spiritual guides in heaven intend that we have knowledge of an existence beyond this physical life.

At the end of our life, our essence reconnects with our soul and we are transported to a beautiful place on the other side. In this place, there is the subtle, white light of the purest love and peace. There is no sickness, no pain, no anger, no disfigurement and our body is perfect. We are transformed. Our soul is now our total existence. All negative thoughts and words have been eradicated and cannot possibly exist in this perfect and loving environment. Our soul holds our lessons, our experiences, and our love.

In this realm of heaven, there is no laziness, no fear, no aggravation and no procrastination. We have duties to accomplish. We have lessons to conclude and new lessons to commence. The lessons are learned in a series of elegant rooms in an exquisite, marble building. Within this building is one room where the souls of people, who have taken their life, are helped and guided with tenderness and compassion. Theirs is a very involved lesson to conclude.

In heaven, we are very social, spending time with each other in positive circumstances. We even bother to search out people we had met only once or twice while on Earth. In our earthly life, we make the effort of a social get-together for those very close to us, but for others, we promise to get together, but rarely does this materialize, since we are so busy with our day-to-day lives. We need to celebrate more while on Earth. We can only appreciate the expense and effort a person has made to host a dinner party, by doing this ourselves for other people. It is fun to get together with a group of people, share food, laugh and enjoy the company of each other, but we do this for ten percent of our time and conduct our job and busy life for ninety percent. In heaven, it is the opposite, where we socialize ninety percent and work for ten percent. Work is not 'work' as we understand it in the earthly sense, but could involve instruction, learning or helping one another. No special spiritual tool is required for us to make this change today to socialize, as we have the capability right now, but we must ascertain whether we have the inclination.

If a person tells you that they are about to take a cruise, you would appreciate that this is a very pleasurable trip. You may have taken a cruise yourself, so are familiar with the food, the entertainment, meeting new people and the laughter. You have been where they are going, so you know they will have a very wonderful time. You might even feel a little envy. This is illustrative of existence on the other side, which is very enjoyable all the time. Our societal perception of death is morbid, a loss, a finality and grief. This is the tone of how we incorporate into our life the loss of a loved one. We feel there is nothing cheerful about it. People, who have departed life, try energetically, however, to get the message to their family on the earthly plane that they are in a good place and are very happy. Were guilt to exist on the other side, they would probably feel guilty that they are very happy and their family on Earth are grieving and tearful. The cheerful existence on the other side makes the concept of death seem remote from the torment that it caused on earth. Death brought the person who departed a release and the continuation of soul evolvement in a perfect environment but brought their family grief, sadness and despair to try to continue living their life wholeheartedly. This is probably the greatest dichotomy within humanity.

Over many years, as my healing work evolved, I found myself journeying more and more to another realm at night. I have visited the marbled building to receive instruction in another area of my work. I have met souls, both departed and still living on Earth, in this marbled building, who have shared their thoughts with me. Some nights, it felt as if I had spent my entire night with a small group of people in one of their houses, talking with them. Each time, it was a different group of people and a different house. This group of people, they usually shared information that was not profoundly sensitive and appeared to be more of a social context. There would usually be one person in that group, dedicated to me, who would lead me to a place to meet the other people. If I met just one person alone, I understood that they needed my assistance in getting a message to a person, who is alive, to help both their souls heal. An example of this was my role in uniting the souls of the young swimmer driving a car, and his friend, who died when the car was involved in an accident.

I did request to meet my family members who have passed, and this wish was granted to me. The reunions were always brief. So strong is the emotion of meeting them again, that I am usually under the impression, upon waking, that they are still alive, until I remember the realm in which I had been around them.

If I were to wake up from a journey and I knew that I was experiencing it, I would request that I return and continue it, which did happen. I would then fall into a deep sleep and continue from the point at which my journey had been interrupted. The ability to journey has refined my capacity to gather information from a person's energy, as I could create a stronger link with the place where the information originated.

Every person can have spiritual experiences, travel to heaven and talk with those departed. It takes the will to let go of our everyday lives and free our mind from those encumbrances. It takes dedication to make numerous attempts until you achieve success.

Occasionally during my personal journeys, I have been asked to keep to myself some of the information which is shared with me. I understand this is the case when the thought is prefaced with the word 'secret', which I take to mean that it is, in fact, a secret. I recognize that this information is for my learning and advancement only, and not intended to be shared. I fully respect and honor this and have incorporated it into my code of ethics. If the word is heard during a healing consult, it implies that I am about to share with the client extremely sensitive information about a traumatic event. I am being alerted so that I might show the greatest compassion while sharing this information.

Effective and thoughtful interaction has been overshadowed to some extent with the advent of personal electronic products into our society. With the opportunity to make purchases with the flick of the wrist, we have become a society of instant gratification. This expectation and sense of entitlement carry over into our home life, workplace and pastimes. It appears to have also carried over into improving our life, where guidance and improvement strategies are appealing only if results can be seen after one hour. The work required to heal our life does not offer rapid results. It would be propagating the notion that people could show up at a healing practice, get their information, implement it that night and see incredible, positive results the next morning. This is not how it happens. I respect the three decades it has taken me to learn my work and the time necessary to prepare for a healing session. There is no instant gratification of the spiritual realm. The effective procedure is for people to advance from one point of evolvement to the next, methodically and purposefully. They will certainly witness encouraging results as they go through this series and the progress made after several healing sessions will be astounding. It is a regeneration of their spirit to allow the rebirth of their soul. They have had the opportunity to incorporate the spiritual coping tools into their life gradually so that the end result will be rational and welcomed. I am very privileged to have many clients in my healing practice, who are following a plan of progressive sessions and they are proud of the effort they are making to empower their life. They can enjoy their results of an improved life.

A lesson, which we are to learn while on this earth, is communication. Good communication is key. Positive communication is the source to avoiding the infiltration of negative aspects into our emotional level. Benefits do not result from angry communication, but only from the positive exchange of communication between people. We certainly want people to communicate with us but we do not always make the effort to do this with others. A person should make a significant effort to communicate. To ignore a positive communication is to be deprived of invigorating energy.

While on the Earth plane, if we do not communicate meaningfully with other people, we can hardly expect to achieve communication with the spiritual realm. With no spiritual communication, we would not be able to acquire healing, especially since we do not understand where it is, what it is or how to reach it. The art of spiritual communication grows out of positive, physical communication on the earthly plane. We know its importance, as we teach our babies words as soon as their brains have created the neural pathways to enable this. We want to and need to understand their needs as we are responsible for their care. Rather than trying to interpret a baby's cry to ascertain their need, we are happy when the baby can finally communicate their need in words. It is, therefore, perplexing to understand why the need for communication then becomes greatly demoted in importance as soon as we have mastered speech.

Many of my clients are estranged from their children. The overwhelming joy that this child brought when they came into the world has now transformed into a total separation from their parent with non-existent communication. The instigator of this estrangement might be the parent or the child. The breakdown of this communication must first be resolved if a solid base is to be formed, on which communication with the spiritual realm can be created.

The demotion of communication is further accentuated in our modern society with the creation and use of cell phones. Sometimes we are not able to talk face to face. Although cell phones are a useful tool for distant communication, they paradoxically carry an opposite action. The cell phone has the provision to 'ignore' a caller. To select the 'ignore' option for a call from a familiar caller is reprehensible if we are able to take the call. This is also true of electronic messaging. When a familiar person sends a message, they anticipate a reply. When no reply is received, the sender might conclude that their friend ignored them as they thought it a waste of their time. Ironically, in avoiding to respond, a message, though an unfavorable one, had in fact been sent. Communication is already known to us on the physical human level but has to be learned by the soul on the spiritual level. We must first form a basis of positive and considerate communication on the human level so that this quality communication can be transferred to and learned by the soul.

Occasionally, people are forced into a situation where they have to communicate with us in sad circumstances. Words are lost to them. People will reach out to console us and say contrived phrases, which are intended to comfort us but do not reach us. The people meant to communicate their support, their sadness, but could not find the precise words to relay this. Their motive was well-intentioned. Until they have lived that specific experience, they do not know what the affected people are feeling or going through. Until they encounter a similar experience, only then will they truly understand and have the words at their disposal to express it.

Many of us will encounter the death of a parent. We live life believing that our parents will always be there for us, invincible, living healthy and vital lives to become centenarians. Then, one day, it changes and a parent passes away. Until this happens in our life, we cannot fully understand it. It is almost as if life initially gave us an illusion to believe in and, as we got older, a different layer revealed itself. We finally saw what lay hidden underneath. It was inevitable and logical, that a parent would pass away before us. This cycle, once it begins, then has to complete and a new cycle will be created. Even though the parent's life had completed, as they had reached a ripe old age, this does not make it easier to accept their departure. The death of a parent generates another phase of our life to commence. We feel alone and the surviving parent feels alone. Together, we begin the next cycle in our lives.

We have life, so we must have death. Death is one concept that will arouse fear in us. I no longer have a fear of death. It is not the end of my life, but the beginning of my new existence. This event will, however, cause sadness to my family and, for that, I feel regret. I have visited heaven, so I truly believe I will merely return there permanently. My visits to the Earth plane will then be different. I will be in spirit form, invisible to my dear ones, with whom I cannot speak as they cannot hear me or sense me. It will almost be a reversal of the situation I presently have, living on Earth and journeying to heaven.

I am not told if a person is about to die. I am, however, given information to deliver, to forewarn them of a distressing time. I passed on such information from a client's departed family member one year before their relative's husband passed away at a young age. The message of concern from the client's family member was to advise the client not to become involved as the aftermath would have caused tremendous stress. The client, who was not close to the relative, heeded the warning and avoided all the calamity which ensued.

Giving information to a client about their death is not my information to give, as that will take away a person's freewill to choose whether to know this information. I am, therefore, given messages and read information in a Soul Healing for absolutely every topic, except death. Even if I might strongly encourage a person to seek medical help and they choose otherwise, resulting in their death, I would not be told of this eventuality. People are fearful to know when they are going to die. People might be afraid to come to my practice to receive a healing, as they believe I might know when they are going to die. They need not have this worry. Respecting that a person is fearful of this, the spiritual realm does not give this information to me, as I am obligated to deliver every message to the client. I do not analyze any of the messages or readings I receive and do pass on all messages verbatim. I have no choice in this, as the information is received by my soul and passed on from my soul, so there is, thankfully, no opportunity for my brain to scrutinize nor discard it.

Psychic mediums, who speak with those departed, receive messages and give them to a person, who then feels a connection to their departed loved one. This is the extent of the receiver's expectation. For the work of healing, the person would hold the belief that they will be healed, cured and healthy after one or two sessions. A misconception exists, as I am not the one who can make them cured. I am merely the intermediary, bringing them the healing energy. The expectation that they will be cured, by facing all the causes of their poor health, is proportionate to their diligence to receive the guidance and do the tasks to attain improved health and a happier life. Being cured is absolutely possible. It can happen simply by their choosing and executing.

God guides me and I guide my family. I also guide the people I work with. 'Guide' is not the same as 'lead'. It is not as lofty as 'lead'. I simply pass on information and energy to help people have a better life. I give people inspiration to do the work to improve their lives. I bring them comfort in the knowledge that everything is possible and, just because they have been tolerating an issue for forty years, does not mean that it cannot be removed from their life permanently. Working at the greatly elevated levels of vibrational energy achieves the most positive results and, if the client is receptive, very impressive outcomes will result to fundamentally improve their life and health.

8
Post-traumatic stress disorder

Post-Traumatic Stress Disorder, or PTSD, once unknown, is now a familiar term. Numerous people have found themselves suffering from PTSD. On the physical level, it can arise as a result of deeply traumatic incidents, involving sexual assault or witnessing acts of brutality in warfare. Veterans returning from active duty found that their service had developed into more than their duty to their country when they also had PTSD to cope with. The continual subjection to witnessing killing, violent acts and inhumanity had seeped deep into their consciousness.

The debilitating reach of this disorder then crept into the lives of the sufferers' loved ones, their families, their sleep and their day-to-day life. It robbed them of the joy of life. It brought them the negative emotions of anger, irritability, hopelessness and depression. PTSD is a social disorder, as it does not leave the afflicted person suffering on his or her own, but encompasses all family members and friends, putting them at risk. The PTSD sufferer may make valiant attempts to enjoy life with their family or friends, but there would be the menace lurking, ready to subvert any joy.

Horrific images continually replay for the sufferer as flashbacks or nightmares, degenerating their quality of life. In the case of military veterans, they had put aside their fear on the battlefield and at their military job, displaying total bravery, but now had to face fear out of context in their daily home life. The fear of these images looming up unannounced could not be halted.

This is the story of a very dear friend of mine, who served in the Armed Forces and now suffers from PTSD. I will call him Dan. He gave a great part of his life of thirty years to serve his country. He was posted in active war zones, where there was fighting, brutality, shootings and landmine explosions. There was a total disregard for humanity, to which he, a person filled with gentleness and kindness, should not have been subjected. His moral compass was inverted. He tried to internalize the distressing experiences, by not recounting to his wife or friends any of the atrocities he had witnessed, in the hope of protecting those people from the very nightmares he had to endure. These images, referred to as a 'flipchart' by Dan, laid repressed and dormant for eighteen years until they re-emerged as brutal, incessant images in his mind every day and night. When trauma exists in the soul, it then seeps into the physical life and colors the way a person experiences situations and behaves. Small, innocent items around Dan's house became cruel triggers to activate the flipchart. Anger and irritability surfaced and became part of his daily behavior. It was a torture as horrifying as that on the battlefield.

Dan began questioning the feelings and behavior he was exhibiting. He suspected these occurrences might be PTSD related and underwent tests. Since his condition matched the majority of the criteria for PTSD, his diagnosis was confirmed. His symptoms included: flashbacks, irritability, angry outbursts, hypervigilance, hopelessness, difficulty concentrating, sleep problems, feeling detached from others and looking for the exit in every room due to insecurity.

His brain, responsible for providing the images of the flipchart, turned on itself and caused anger in him. The emergence of this aggression was his coping mechanism for the violent flashbacks. This impacted his family around him. There were no longer good and bad days but a stretch of consistently bad days, for himself and therefore for his family. When he sought rest or rejuvenating sleep, the images started to play and did not permit him to replenish his energy, depleting it still further. He had minimal energy for the next day. Dan's focus was directed to mere survival in this new mode of life. Sheer survival meant that he could not entertain the remotest possibility that life could improve.

Dan had witnessed inhumane acts in his role as a soldier. This had created immense guilt, which now existed in his soul. He could not comprehend that man was capable of these brutalities and a fear arose because he had seen that it was possible. The fear was heightened as he felt that, as an observer and even participator, he was also a contributor as he had been unable to prevent the brutality. This extremely deep-seated fear existed within him, in his soul. This is a fear, which hopefully most of us will never encounter. Due to the guilt, the fear and the anger, numerous pieces of Dan's soul energy fled. He began seeking help from medical doctors and psychologists, many of whom have never experienced PTSD emotions firsthand but instead applied procedures they had gleaned from the accounts of other PTSD sufferers or from medical journals. The medical doctors were approaching their treatment from the physical level to find the solution in the mental level of the patient. That is not where the issue exists.

Dan did not want to be changed in the way he was changed. He looks at the positives, as that is his gentle personality; he is grateful he did not suffer debilitating physical maiming. He visits his friends in the veteran hospital and feels guilt that he is able to live at home and they have not only been mentally altered but also physically maimed. He carried guilt from this. He reasoned that he was not as badly off as he had thought until the turning pages of the flipchart reminded him once again of his own personal nightmares. He became a prisoner of himself with no escape from himself.

Due to the hypersensitivity of PTSD sufferers, they become very uncomfortable if other people's energy overlaps with their energy and feel that their energy is being assaulted. Anxiety grows from this. In a subconscious way to protect themselves from this assault, they alienate themselves and begin to mistrust others. Isolated, they avoid and then lose interest in activities and then in life. Hopelessness sets in. Their expectation of a normal life is now too remote.

Dan credits the strength of his wife and children in preventing him from hurting himself or taking his own life, as so many of his colleagues had done. Many soldiers, who had survived war, could not survive the return to their civilian life. It took courage for Dan to knowingly make the decision not to take his life and thereby inflict more pain and heartache on his already heartbroken family.

This was the resilience of this amazing man. He exhibited a dire survival, firstly for his family's sake, then for his own sake. This took more valor than he had ever displayed on the battlefield. This drive to accomplish is usually taught to us by our parents, but it is also an innate virtue of the soul. Not every person has access to this drive. Dan, being quite spiritual, was rudimentarily linking with his soul by accessing energy at higher levels, though he was not even aware he was doing this.

The person with PTSD must firstly be ready and willing to be healed before healing can occur. This might appear self-evident, but causes apprehension for some sufferers, as access to their energy is required. They would have to give the healer permission and make a commitment. They are afraid of the horrors they might have to relive in order to address and eradicate the issues. This fear blocks them from attempting to get any help. They have endured this disorder for so long, that it has now formulated their personality and they have significantly adapted their daily life to accommodate it. Their fear has morphed into a fear of releasing their accustomed fear as it has now defined them. They cling to this state of mind, even though this translates into a problematic life and could ultimately manifest into a serious illness. Drawing aside this mesh that shrouds their issues must be done in order to present the full understanding of the trauma. The benefit of Soul Healing is that there is not the need to relive the trauma, but only to see its energy to enable the respective energy pieces to be welcomed and received into the soul. No emotional pain from the trauma is experienced during healing, but only compassion, peace and healing. With the retrieval of each energy piece, the fear would be de-activated. With the acceptance of all the energy pieces, the Soul Healing would be completed. Dan had already taken the initial step, as he was open-minded to the possibility of receiving healing.

When my husband and I visited Dan last year, I gifted him my first book and asked him to read it to prepare his soul by using the images and colors of the book to connect to the highest vibrational levels of energy. I explained that it was possible to conduct my healing work remotely. Whether it was out of desperation or a lack of remaining options beyond traditional medical practices, he welcomed the prospect of receiving healing energy remotely.

Prior to contacting Dan, I spent a lot of time reading his energy. I was shown numerous images to give me the information to begin the healing for Dan. We were three thousand miles apart, so healings were conducted by telephone. We began phoning each other every three days for one month. This was with the intention of creating momentum in the progress made and so Dan could gain confidence in the process and in himself. During our first telephone conversation, I asked Dan to summarize how he felt this disorder had affected him, his life and his family. He spoke of the anger he felt with everything, his disappointment that he had to deal with these emotions, the sadness that his family was suffering as a result of his suffering and the inability to sleep, thus making it difficult to function the next day. He was tortured with constant flashbacks and nightmares. His life was a mess. He could not stop the downward spiralling. It had bled the happiness from his life. He had a strong marriage of thirty years with an incredible lady. She was his main support, even when times were very challenging for her. The doctors and psychologists had been trying various methods to zap the images, leaving his brain assaulted and affecting his speech and movement. I was personally saddened by what my friend was going through. Deep scars are sometimes left in the brain from attempting to heal trauma on the physical level. Through Soul Healing, there is no scar left and all is renewed, so I was determined to bring him the healing he needed, but it would be up to him if the healing would be effective. If there was a time when I was glad that I worked at the soul level and did not have the overwhelmingly sad emotions to deal with from being personally invested, this was it.

During a phone call, I explained to Dan about my work, energy, the process of a healing and how to heal the soul. I wanted him to understand that I was not simply doing something to someone, but that he would be doing this work for himself and I was merely the intermediary. This basis of understanding helped him to feel reassured about receiving and accepting healing.

During our phone calls, Dan was encouraged to get out of his head, to switch off his brain and quieten the flipchart. The brain cannot solve this disorder, as the plane on which the true issue lies cannot be reached from the brain. Attempting to handle this with the brain is futile, as this would result in merely dealing with the symptoms, not the cause. Only the soul is able to manage this causal issue profoundly and effectively. The soul is able to eradicate the traumatic images without Dan ever needing to see them. The suppressed images would be represented by a blank white square during a Soul Healing.

The remote healings of clearing were conducted with soothing background music. The meditations were guided by my commentary and background music. The Soul Healings were conducted to music only. I could not communicate during the Soul Healing as I was functioning totally from my soul and speech to Dan would have involved activating my brain. Dan patiently accepted the silence and allowed the healing energy to reach him remotely. These methods proved very beneficial for Dan, as he had the opportunity to release some very difficult emotions. Exercises, which enabled Dan to think outside of his body and to get out of the brain, were conducted. This was done through several meditations of visualizing white light. Focusing on this light, allowed the brain to switch off and the soul to begin to guide, locate the energy of the images and eradicate it. Initially, the healings were healings of clearing and release, after which they were conducted for the profound healing from the trauma through Soul Healings and Dynamic Soul Healings.

At first, Dan had difficulty in visualizing white light. He was trying to imagine it, rather than visualize it, and was thus using his brain and not his soul. The difference is that, through imagination, we create the image in our brain, whereas, when we visualize, the soul brings us the image to view. Unfortunately, the male brain is wired physiologically to operate primarily from the left hemisphere, therefore very logically, so ethereal concepts are sometimes slightly out of reach. This does not imply that this is impossible for a male to attain, but that some innovation is required to shut off the brain and implement full visualization. I tried various concepts to help Dan with visualization and found one to which he could relate. He could visualize a beam of white light rather than white light flowing down through the crown chakra. He also found the image of the beam relaxing, so was also visualizing this while falling asleep.

He was given the tool of visualizing a burst of brilliant white light over the flipchart as soon as it began to creep in. He was very adept at doing this. The flipchart was still appearing but less frequently. He successfully learned an exercise of visualizing a blue ocean, blue sky and a white sphere on the horizon. The white sphere was a way to visualize white light and represented his soul. The ocean also had a secondary level of benefit by simultaneously presenting the healing power of water and Dan readily absorbed this energy. With each successive phone call, a greater degree of progress was being made.

Visualizing white light entering the crown chakra was still eluding Dan. He could not see white light around him and sometimes saw himself in brown or grey, also being the colors of camouflage. This was due to the interference from the brain, deflecting Dan from seeing himself surrounded by white. It was a latent emotion of believing he was not worthy of being surrounded by white, only by sombre colors. It was essential that he succeeded in seeing white light drifting into his crown chakra, as this prompted the soul to take over from the brain. He wanted this so intensely, that he was overthinking the process. We did meditations to quieten the exertion of his brain so that the process could become a natural one. This was partially successful as he could visualize the light, but it still did not descend towards him. Progress was being made in baby steps.

The frequency of phone calls was reduced to every two weeks for two months, to afford Dan the opportunity to use by himself the tools he had learned. At our next phone call, Dan advised that he could fall asleep and stay asleep. This gave him more energy to function the next day. Since the number of occasions of seeing the flipchart had vastly decreased, he was able to handle each instance by immediately seeing a burst of white light over it, thereby eliminating it. The power of the flipchart was diminishing. Dan was in control, determining what he allowed himself to see or think. This was key. Initially, the intrusive thoughts had power over him, determining how he would react. After the healings and meditations, the balance definitely shifted to Dan reclaiming control.

Our next phone call was six weeks later. Being a diligent student, Dan had not only maintained using all the tools but had made great progress. It was a watershed for him. At night, he was falling asleep immediately, staying asleep until early morning and falling back to sleep. He was feeling relaxed and had much more energy to enjoy his day. The flipchart was appearing very infrequently and he was able to zap it, or at least to pause it. His doctor had reduced his medications. He felt positive about his progress.

As symptoms were removed or brought under control with the healing of the causal issue, it revealed more clearly any remaining issue. Dan talked about a concern, of which he had not been aware until it was revealed when other issues had been eradicated. As dusk approached and the house became engulfed in dim light, he would begin to feel despondent and would switch on many house lights. His duty as a soldier involved patrolling at night, making him vulnerable to attack, so he was fearful when he had to perform this duty. The natural transition of day to night was now a trigger for this fear. An innocent process of nature had brought him a distress to deal with. I conducted a Dynamic Soul Healing to release the emotions of vulnerability and fear. It was crucial that he felt safe in his home.

When our phone calls had first begun, Dan had many of the symptoms of PTSD: flashbacks, nightmares, aggression, detachment, hypervigilance, mistrust, hopelessness and the inability to sleep. Due to his consistent dedication to utilizing the tools and taking control, some symptoms were eradicated or greatly reduced after seven months. No symptom remained at the full force of its initial effect. When Dan was asked how his life had changed over the past year, he told me that he was getting a better sleep so could function more effectively the next day; the flipchart was popping up infrequently and he could control it by using white light to delete it; he could go amongst a crowd and not feel too anxious; he does not constantly look for the exit when in a room; day turning into night still prompts him to turn on the house lights, but the dire anxiety had reduced; he was not feeling as constantly fearful as he once did. His wife said she had not seen him smile so much in a very long time.

The Soul Healings had helped Dan by greatly diminishing the power of the causal issues and this greatly reduced many of his symptoms. Initially, the healings were a coping mechanism, but then they became the solution. This ultimately unmasked all the symptoms and all issues were healed at the source. Dan no longer had as many PTSD-related emotions to suppress. We had located them, acknowledged them and released them. Of course, he could bring back any of the symptoms, but he was determined that he would no longer provide the energy foundation to nurture them.

It was rewarding for me that, however the phone calls were spaced in time, Dan never forgot any of the phone call appointments and phoned exactly at that time. This showed me that this was important to him and it was successful for him for this reason. It took tremendous trust for Dan to allow me to put him through connecting with the energy of the traumatic incidents so that the energy pieces could be retrieved, welcomed, received and accepted. His soul was healed from the PTSD trauma. His courage brought him the positive results.

This spring, Dan will be visiting to receive three site healings. After this, it is expected that Dan will have none of the negative emotions, the flashbacks, the hypervigilance or the fear. This energy will be replaced with happiness, enjoying time with his wife, children and grandchildren and working on his hobbies. He can reclaim the joy of his life.

His life path will bring him to bringing healing to others. He has experienced the brutal reality of war and its aftermath so that he can speak from the experience of truly knowing what sufferers with PTSD face. He will bring hope to others by describing how he handled and eradicated his symptoms. Other people will be healed as a result. This will be the power of the soul.

9
The first domino

The concept of the 'first domino' implies that, when several dominos are placed upright and close together in a row and should the first one fall over, it would topple onto the second domino. The pair would then cascade forward onto the third domino and so on. Only when all dominos have been knocked over, would the process end.

This can be applied as an analogy for the health of a person, who begins taking medication for an issue with a vital organ. There are usually side-effects, invariably affecting another organ and this necessitates taking another pill to resolve that issue. The first domino has fallen onto the second. As more side effects occur affecting other organs and more pills are prescribed, the second and third dominoes fall, and so on. A person could find themselves taking several pills a day. A dramatic increase of chemical in the bloodstream would overwhelm the circulatory system and kidneys, detrimentally affecting muscles and ultimately their mobility. All dominoes have toppled over. Although this is an oversimplification of the care of a person's health, it is presented to illustrate how their health can spiral down, when the well-intentioned, initial treatment was planned to make them well again.

In western medicine, there are specialists for each of the organs and systems in the body. When a person has an issue with a specific organ, their physician will refer them to that particular specialist. Many separate appointments with the various specialists could be created if a person is having issues with more than one vital organ. Each specialist begins treatment without an exact diagnosis, sometimes working from the standpoint of ruling out causes within that organ. This adds another layer of complexity, as this method might impact other organs, unintentionally causing further complications to the patient's health. The specialist is looking to at least eliminate the symptoms of their specific organ and not necessarily to ascertain the root cause, which could ostensibly be situated in a different organ. This is, of course, all well-intentioned, as the doctor's fundamental concern is to help their patient. I have every respect for the medical profession's challenging work, as this is how I began my journey of discovering the best method to help people live healthier lives.

It is rarely the case that only one single domino will fall. It is usually the situation that once the first domino falls, there is no stopping the downward spiral of a person's health. A specialist might be at the sixth 'domino' trying to fix it from their own perspective, whereas the optimum approach would be to look at the first 'domino' and determine how it could have been prevented from falling. It would involve treating the cause, not the symptom. This is the approach of traditional eastern medicine, which is utilized in the healthcare systems of Japan and China, promoting a healthier population and vastly reducing visits to the doctor's office.

Ideally, we could heal ourselves and eliminate all doctor's office visits, or, at the very least, drastically reduce the visits. Although this might appear as an extremist view, it is a goal we should strive towards. People should be encouraged to educate themselves to take care of their own health, rather than hand this over to a stranger, albeit a medically qualified stranger. Doctors are essential in assisting a person to have tests and scans to ascertain a condition, to arrange and perform surgery or to make additional assistance available to a person. It is the western healthcare system, which is falling short for patient care, not the doctors themselves. The doctors are as entangled in this convoluted system as the patients themselves.

I am proud that I practise what I preach. My family and I enjoy good health. I attribute this to receiving new energy each morning from the higher levels, appreciating the many blessings in my life, nutritious food, laughter and spending time outside in the sunshine. I believe in preventative care, so I am attentive to my family's health, immediately eliminating any issue so that it is not afforded the opportunity to develop into a serious condition.

With present-day access to a wide range of products, people's good health faces challenges of our own making. Each year brings an increased number of people who have been diagnosed with cancer and other debilitating diseases. On the physical level, it is acknowledged that cancer will materialize in the body through smoking cigarettes, exposing skin to the hot sun, the mineral of talc in some products used for personal hygiene, ingesting chemicals used in some processed foods and drinking the substances used in flavoring some soft drinks. Societal pressures have also contributed to eating disorders by causing young girls and boys to aspire to reflect the perfect body image depicted in magazines. As well as initiating eating disorders, such as anorexia nervosa or bulimia, eating a narrow range of foods causes the blood to become more acidic and may be a cause of cancer. When an entire food group, such as starches and fats, is eliminated from the diet in order to lose weight, this puts stresses on the cells, causing them to mal-form and can also lead to cancer.

In the same way as a car needs a variety of fluids in the engine and supporting systems to run, our body needs the complete range of the food groups to fabricate the nutrients required to nourish the entire body. Today, we have the option of eating a healthier version in all the food groups, so it is possible to still eat from all the food groups.

On the spiritual level, cancer has occurred as a result of harboring deep fear, where a person has no outlet to release it or no knowledge of how to eradicate it. People, in today's society, are bombarded with notions of greater expectations and many feel this is unreachable, creating within them the fear that they are a failure. If this energy is retained at the spiritual level, it will increase and manifest into cancer of the physical body. We know why cancer happens. We do not, however, strive to purposely remove the causes or adjust behavior in the causal situations and so we continue to flounder in our endeavors to treat the resulting cancer. It appears that, once the cancer has spread and taken control of the body, it is the belief that it is a futile effort to abate it. This might be due to the strength of the cancer cells or the weakened resistance from the body, or both. The word 'terminal' becomes part of the terminology spoken by the medical staff. The end result is definitive in that it terminates a person's life.

Years ago, we were able to attribute the occurrence of cancer to the body aging thus losing resistance to fight it. This initiated the body's inability to generate new cells or to regenerate expended cells. Today, this theory no longer holds true, with the critical increase in the prevalence of cancer in young children. It is unfathomable that a six-year-old body could develop cancer, but, unfortunately, there are many such cases. Cigarettes are obviously not the cause, so we must look to the food. It is indeed a dichotomy that food, the very substance which is supposed to sustain our body and life, could be the very thing which is harming us.

We continue to expose ourselves to the same causes of cancer, repeat the same medical procedures, continuously conduct research to discover new though incomplete answers, lose our loved ones at a young age and wonder why we cannot exit this cycle. So long as people continue to smoke cigarettes, breathe in and ingest chemicals and allow the sun to heat their unprotected skin, the development of cancer cells cannot be prevented. Compound this with the deep-seated fear people harbor within themselves, and the inevitable end result is cancer. Fundamental changes must be made in order to achieve fundamentally new and positive results. The causes of cancer exist and because we are reluctant to renounce the causal activities, we submit ourselves to allowing the cancer cells to freely subsist and continue to claim new patients daily. A solution to cancer does exist, but we are looking in the wrong places. The solution has already been discovered in the spiritual realm and needs to be transferred to the physical level where it can be the solution to cancer and rescue and heal many people.

Magnetism has a powerful effect. Bioelectromagnetism has the ability to change the composition of living cells. If harnessed correctly, magnetism could be used to draw out cancer cells by causing them to cluster together. As a batch, their ability to flow through the lymphatic system is hindered. This cluster is also a large enough target to be manageably destroyed using concentrated magnetism. The presence of magnetism curbs any further spread of cancer cells. This now makes it feasible for the body's defense mechanisms and immune system to regain power and eradicate the remnants of any cancer cells.

The energy within magnetism is even more powerful than the magnetism itself. During a healing, I will see in a person an area of sticky energy, which is causing an energy blockage and impeding energy flow. It could also be the indication of a sick vital organ, as the stuck energy could have already manifested on the physical level. This stickiness is a type of energy magnetism and is not positive for the person. In such a case, I will retrieve energy from higher levels and align its vibration to become magnetic to match the magnetism of the tacky energy. This powerful magnetized energy infiltrates, breaking up the stickiness, whereby it will shrivel away. The body itself has its own therapeutic magnetism and the influx of the new energy will stimulate the body's magnetism to clear up any affected cells. The body holds this power and we need only to activate it.

The body continually produces its own magnetism, which, if exposed to elements of chemicals, may cause deformation and uncontrollable growth rather than the production of healthy cells. Magnetism produced by the body cells can also be influenced by the earth's magnetism or external sources of magnetism, such as power lines, cell phone towers, computers or cell phones. This interaction of the body's magnetism and the chaotic magnetism of our environment usually has a very detrimental effect on the human physiology and therefore our overall health.

It has been shown that a small portion of the body's cells are cancerous, but do not have the opportunity to propagate, as the body's defense mechanism detects genomic irregularities and constantly annihilates them. If the conditions change and the body's defense mechanism is compromised through exposure to cigarette smoke, chemicals, ultraviolet rays from the sun or electromagnetic radiation from electronic screens, cancer cells would have the opportunity to propagate.

We have choices at our disposal. We can choose to use a preventative approach by proactively avoiding any element or action which has been shown to cause cancer or other debilitating diseases. We can destress and relax more, thereby not affording a welcoming energy for fear to establish. This will avert the first domino from falling.

Eastern medicine presents the theory of preventative treatment. The four levels of traditional Tibetan or Ayurvedic healing is the world's oldest whole-body healing process. As Tibetan medicine evolved, it encompassed the best features of the healing methods of other Eastern civilizations. The now familiar catchword 'holistic' has been applied to this method of healing. It is based on the belief that total health is a manifestation of the delicate balance of the physical, mental, emotional and spiritual levels. As the life-force energy of the four levels combines, it causes unique biochemical changes in the body, which heighten its intrinsic ability to heal a wide range of disorders. The combination of this natural ability with herbal medicine, acupuncture, detoxification and rejuvenation offers the advantage of a non-invasive treatment method.

We can explore these types of non-invasive healing systems or simply look to ourselves. One simple healing system we carry within us is laughter. We all have the capacity to laugh. Laughter not only makes us feel very happy, but it stimulates the production of T-cells and immunoglobulins, which are specialized immune cells to fight abnormal cells and pathogen. Medical case studies have shown that laughter reinforces the attack on cancer by increasing the body's levels of Interferon-gamma. We conveniently carry our own medicine and immunity, but it only works if you use it. I grew up in a household of people, who loved to embellish a simple tale into the most epically funny story. I have felt the positive effects of laughter firsthand and value it very much. I have endeavored to pass on this 'medicine' of laughter to my children. They have also developed a marvelous sense of humor, so carry their own medicine. Much to my family's amusement, I will seek to derive even more benefits from the same funny story, by repeating it to myself several times and laughing each time. Laughter can be added to our collection of natural defenses.

A natural practice for maintaining personal well-being, which is readily accessible to us, is to be out in nature. Nature uplifts us and heightens our senses. This can take place in one's own garden. The singing of birds inspires in calming the mind and relaxing the body. A small fountain with the sound of flowing water will bring the healing energy of water around us. Within this supportive environment, however, there are issues caused by seemingly innocuous objects, which need to be addressed. In my modality of Feng Shui Healing, I am acutely aware that the placement of trees around a home can potentially have drastic effects on its occupants. A tree being too close to the house could cause illnesses, especially of the head. On a physical basis, a tree's roots can create an obstruction with the water pipes of the house, causing reduced water flow to the house. This would manifest into energy hindering incoming money to the household. On a spiritual basis, the invading roots at the house wall can affect the energy of all occupants and impede their progress in life.

The health of the trees on or near our property must be monitored. If a tree is situated near the house and is rotting, this will affect the brain of the senior male of the house, causing Alzheimer's, ALS motor neuron disease or Parkinson's disease. A diseased tree will release that contaminated energy to be carried to the occupants, causing them to develop cancer or other debilitating diseases. Essentially, the disease of the tree becomes the disease of the occupants. Although it is regrettable to remove a tree, this is the only solution. If a tree is rotting, then only the rotten portions need to be removed, but a diseased tree must be totally taken out. The energy in that place should then be cleared and blessed so that this energy is completely neutralized and can have no further detrimental effect. If the rotten or diseased tree is not dealt with, this will create the circumstances to cause the first domino to fall.

We are subjected to many hazards in our daily life and must remain constantly alert to avoid or neutralize them. It takes some effort to do this, but, if the end result is good health and the ability to enjoy an enjoyable life, then it is worthwhile to take the time each day to do this. This is all in the endeavor to prevent that first domino from falling.

10
Reading and healing the soul

I have followed my life path and it brought me to discovering healing. This developed into reading and healing the soul. This evolution revealed that the soul holds all our secrets to living a happy and fulfilled life. I enjoy unravelling mysteries to discover what exists beyond the known, so I continued to explore. I was given an awareness of this at three months old when my sister passed away and it has never ceased. At the age of five, I first became cognizant of my unique perspective of being able to see outside of the physical and this has helped bring success to my work of healing.

When people know they are about to die, whether of natural causes or an impending disaster, they have one last thought. It is always about love. "I love you". We all want love. Many of us find love, the love of another person, the love of a child, the love of a pet. We are hopeful and we are optimistic. We have trust in the authenticity of the love we have found with another person. If all the facts indicate that this is the right person, then we trust this and commit our life to them, in marriage or cohabitation.

For those fortunate people, who find a happy and nurturing love, they discover that they must work at maintaining the integrity of their love, as a couple or as a family, but this is not a burden to them. They willingly put in the effort, as the benefits of caring and being cared for are worthwhile. They do not need the impetus of doom when their life is about to end, to prompt them to reach a phone to say "I love you". They have been saying this to their special people all their life. We should all reach out, readily and often, to tell a person we love them and not have a catastrophe propel us to do this. To carry the gentle energy of love within us is extraordinarily beneficial.

I am very blessed in my life to have the love of an incredible husband for over twenty-five years, a family of three children and siblings. My husband and I are best friends, still very happy and we have grown older together, fulfilling all those clichés in romantic movies! Having him in my life makes me readily believe in soul mates and that specific souls belong together.

The subject of love is around us constantly. We hear it as a recurring theme in songs. The lyrics, describing a yearning to love, awaken our own yearning. We long to live the lyrics of a love found to last forever. We buy into this and then we attempt to enact it. Many people are successful in having the triumph of finding true love. They can live the rest of their life with this person and bring each other happiness. For many other people, the discovery of a person to love is an easy step, compared to the task of maintaining that love with them. All too often, it fails, as is shown by the very high divorce rate in the western world. The radical transformation from the vows of overflowing love at the wedding altar to the disparaging words screamed at each other after only two years of marriage kills their dream of true love. It is astounding that such a drastic transmutation is possible. Since we, as caring beings, crave companionship and love, it is sad that we all do not have the triumph to find and sustain love. We all want love so ardently, yet the divorce rate is high due to the lack of effort to continually maintain a happy relationship. Having suffered failure in love impacts our confidence in our ability to find it again. We feel vulnerable, so we do not wish to even pursue it.

Fear has crept in and then begins to send out tentacles to grab a firm hold of our internal emotions. We do not realize that we are inviting this unwelcome energy. It seats itself within us and begins to dictate our reactions to events similar to the event which created it. We are now afraid to love. We keep our distance. We cannot commit. If we are wronged by another person, we have an overreaction and conclude this with ostracizing the individual, even if it is our adult child or our sibling. We justify not contacting them ever again. The issue, which caused it, is seldom remembered, but our reaction to it and the ostracization of the person is vehemently preserved.

Many clients, who come to see me, have a family member, whom they have alienated. They recite numerous reasons to justify this situation. They cling to this energy so fervently, that I am unable to perform a complete release of this energy. As a first step, they are assigned the task of attempting to talk with the person. This task would, however, need to be done totally at the physical level, the brain. It is a necessary first step, after which I am able to extract the hostile energy within them since they are now more likely to surrender it.

Such is the battle within the family unit. Some people have this battle within themselves. This relates to their ego. This is not in the sense of having a grandiose opinion of themselves. This relates to the Greek word 'I'. Each of us has this energy within us. Ego wants to control events and life to go the way as it deems appropriate. This triggers our gut feeling as a safety mechanism of balance. A great tug of war can ensue between our ego and our gut feeling. It is no wonder that people are confused and indecisive. The energy of our ego needs to be located and the vibration lowered, so that it still functions, but not at the dominating level.

A person is able to act or react only within the realm of their experience. This can cause conflict between a parent and child, where the parent's realm is so much more extensive and they are trying to pass on this benefit to their child. The same situation, which a young child experienced, can be seen in a very different light when that child becomes older and wiser. Their realm of experience has extended and enabled them to see the situation with experienced eyes.

We learn life lessons a block at a time, sequence by sequence: as a baby, as a toddler, as a child, as a young man or woman, as an adult, as a spouse, as a parent, as a wage earner. We cannot, much as we would like to, overtake our parents' exposure to experience and knowledge of life before we have earned it. We must dutifully follow after. We can, however, lead in front of our own children or younger acquaintances. A parent has known their child within the family unit all his or her life, so has complete knowledge of the child's entire life. The child does not have the knowledge of the entire life of the parent and is only aware of the portion of the parent's life which overlaps with their own.

Within the framework of these blocks of learning, we develop our personalities. It is intriguing that our personalities are each unique. A person might laugh a lot, but so do millions of other people. It is an exceptional intrinsic creation, whereby each one of those millions, who laughs, is still different from another person as each has a unique laugh. When all these unique laughs come together to produce a chorus of laughter, it is very uplifting. All that uniqueness and differences blend into a harmony, creating a oneness. Every laughing crowd sounds very similar. We can sit in an audience, watching a comedian on stage. At each punch line, we all laugh together and enjoy it, even though he might sometimes be gently mocking our behavior in life.

There is also a distinction in our voice. Vocal chords, a larynx and air combine to produce a unique voice in each one of us. We can recognize a person from their voice without seeing them. This vocal uniqueness transfers into the singing voice, when we can identify the singer on the radio from their voice. There is no instrument of voice in the spiritual realm. Energy is used and this is received as energy by the medium, who then translates it into the vocal sounds of words using their own voice. Our family members, who have crossed over, will retain the characteristics of the voice they had on Earth so that the medium could describe this and we could identify them.

I conduct spiritual work on both the spiritual and universal levels. Messages received from souls connected to the client originate from energy on the spiritual level. When working with healing information, this is received at the universal level, where the highest vibrational levels of energy exist. I receive words as energy. I allow the spiritual level to use fewer words, but sufficient to give me the sense of the message. This is so that their energy can be conserved and enable them to send me more messages. For me, this means that I have to work harder to meet this energy and deliver the information to the person with whom I am working. It is a skill that had to be developed.

A person, who has lost their eyesight, could be an analogy for understanding the relationship between the earthly plane and the universal plane. A person, who was born blind, cannot understand color, never having seen it. They can feel shapes, but this is missing the concept of color. It is difficult to ascertain what they see in their mind's eye. To describe color to them is challenging. Also challenging is how the blind person can describe their perception of a color. This is a correlation to what we see on the spiritual plane and on the Earth plane. I can describe what I see on the spiritual plane, but my listener will, most likely, interpret it by relating it to something with which they are familiar on the Earth plane. I have seen sights in the spiritual realm, which are extremely challenging to articulate relative to anything earthly.

During a healing, I observed that people achieve relaxation at varying degrees of depth. There is no right or wrong way to this. Whichever way works for that individual is appropriate. I work with the energy around them, within them and beyond them. I read this energy, visualizing scenes and hearing words. To maintain the integrity of all this information, I work with a crystal at my wrist during a healing, enabling me to clear away energy immediately, while receiving new information. This enables me to do two or more actions simultaneously, while maintaining the purity of the energy, to bring the full truthfulness of each message. Crystal is a perfect medium for transmitting energy in bidirectional clearing and receiving.

The visualizations and words I receive are clues to the trauma, which has happened in the clients' lives. I share all the information I receive. After a healing, I describe simple tools for the person to use to reinforce the effectiveness of the healing. An example of a tool before sleep is to transmit white light through the crown chakra to clear the brain. As it passes down through the body, it will pick up any irritations or anxieties accumulated during the day and discard them through the soles of the feet. Released of all these agitations, a person will have a restful night's sleep.

The success of a healing is very evident. I performed a healing for a family member, who had taken prescription medication for acid reflux daily for ten years. I located the knot of energy, which manifested as stress, did one healing per week for three weeks and suggested tools to use to keep the stress at bay. The next month, no pills were needed. Today, they are free of acid reflux. These sessions took place three years ago.

People might sometimes believe that moving a couple of items around in their home per Feng Shui will suddenly give them a great life and happiness. If that were the case, we would all be happy, but we are not. We lack some, if not all, of the elements of life: happy marriage or relationship, good health, a strong family unit, a meaningful purpose in life or sufficient money. We are in need of some of these components since it necessitates much more than adjusting an item or introducing a color to generate attaining them. Placing certain elements in a zone in our home to enhance that zone, is like giving vitamins and water to a plant and then just not watering it; it gives the plant a boost of growth but it cannot be developed. Making these modifications in the home is where the adjustment begins, not ends. It takes great control of our will, positive intention and constant reinforcement to supplement the lacking elements of our life and foster greater fulfillment.

A person should not be lazy to progress their life. You can have many excuses, although you might present them as supporting reasons. You cannot get ahead when you cannot even keep up. Change how to keep up, so that it frees you to have the time and energy to improve your life and then to move ahead.

The immediate gratification advertising in society has created the expectation of instant gratification in our daily life. People have an expectation about healing. The benefits of healing should be compared to learning a language. It takes some time to learn the basis to the understanding of a language, so not too much is accomplished in one hour. With perseverance in building on the learning, a person will be able to speak the language quite adequately after a short time. So it is with the learning of the healing language.

Life is not a race. There is time for enjoyment, for reflection, as well as learning. It is certainly not all a chore. A well-known phrase states that life is a journey, not a destination. 'Journey' and 'Life' are analogous terms. If you allow yourself the time to observe the road of your journey, you will notice many miraculous events. I have tried to allow myself time to reflect on the journey of my life and thus have the opportunity to enjoy it. Consequently, I have been fortunate enough to have witnessed many special experiences.

Some twenty-two years ago, after visiting our children's grandparents, my husband and I were taking a flight home with our two children of three years old and one year old. The day before, my husband, not taking his tall frame into account, had injured his neck by hitting his head on the roof of the rental car while getting in. Although he had seen a chiropractor, the neck was immobile and he was in pain. He was stoically trying to get through the airport procedure and wanted to help with the children, but he was suffering. Visually, he appeared fine, although he was keeping quiet as it was painful. We arrived at the gate and as we waited to board, I prayed to God to help us get through this, to take away my husband's pain and for me to be able to look after my babies without my husband's usual help. As I looked up, I saw a tall, striking woman, immaculately dressed with a coiffure of red hair, walk up to the counter.

We boarded. Our seats were at the very back of the plane, with my husband sitting across the aisle from me. As I arrived, the stunning lady was already seated at the window and my seat was beside her. She was welcoming and pleasant. During the flight, she introduced herself as Justeen. She mentioned that she was sorry that my husband had been hurt, although she had not talked to him across the aisle to discover this fact. She wanted to hold my eldest daughter, who insisted on playing with her skirt belt. She happily undid the belt and handed it to my daughter, who was mesmerized by the white reflecting stones.

When the meals were served, Justeen accepted it, but it remained untouched on the pulldown tray. She occupied herself with talking with my eldest daughter. Justeen insisted on holding my younger daughter during the descent. The baby calmed down in her arms. She told me, "You must raise your daughters to be strong, capable women". I thanked her for helping me look after the children since it would have been very difficult without her help. As we walked along the aisle to disembark, I turned back to thank her again. I could not see her over the line of people. I stood at the aircraft door and waited. She did not emerge. I saw the captain and crew exit, so concluded that there were no more passengers on board. I looked in the terminal, by the baggage carousel, but she did not show up. Much as she had appeared in immediate answer to my prayer, so she disappeared after her work was done. There was only one explanation. I wrote about her in my daughters' journals and now they are grown up, they know they have been touched and held by an Angel.

Twenty-two years later, I believe we have honored her request of raising strong, capable women. My daughters have professional careers and an independent spirit to explore, travel and speak before a group. They are delightful people to know.

Had I only known that I had been sitting beside an Angel for four hours, what I could have asked! She was trying so hard to tell me things, about my daughters, my husband, without disclosing too much. Usually, Angels are not permitted to volunteer information, but to act only in response to our request for information. She probably said more than she should have; this was probably why they sent a feisty Angel! My brain, however, was consumed with looking after two babies and an injured husband, so I was operating totally on the brain level when I should have been experiencing this from my soul. I would then have been aware that I was in the presence of, and had the opportunity to speak with, an Angel and ask for the information I have always wanted to know. I have since made up for that missed opportunity with numerous exchanges with the Angelic realm.

In case I ever felt that my son had missed out on this incredible experience, as he had not yet been born when his sisters met the Angel, he was given his own experience. He was fifteen months old when I had taken him out in his stroller for a Mother's Day celebration. After the event, while going to the car in the parking lot, I saw a young man, about twenty years old, dressed in shorts and a t-shirt, who was forming something out of balloons. We were the only people around, so I went up to him. He was very pleasant and handsome with blond hair and blue eyes. He immediately paid attention to my son, making an animal for him out of white balloons. As he did so, I observed him. His hair was perfect, his face was perfect, his skin was perfect, his clothes were perfect, even his short white socks were perfect. He did not seem real. Of course, looking back on this encounter, I realized that this was my first clue! He gave the balloon animal to my son. He took out a perfect, red apple and bit into it. He chatted about the importance of Mother's Day. I was impressed with his kind words in honoring mothers. I thanked him and we left. There were no other people around. While I was placing my son into the car, I looked back. There was no trace of the young man. There was a tall wire fence surrounding the area, so the only way out was for him to pass by us and he did not do that. I smiled and told my son that one day, I would tell him this special story.

I recorded this encounter in my son's journal. Today, my son is a tall, very handsome and respectful young man. We still have the white balloon animal, although it has lost some air in twenty years. I have no doubt at all that we met an Angel that day. My soul was open to connecting with an Angel. My essence was willing to accept the encounter. When a person is aware of the magnificence, which lies beyond them, the soul opens up. Incredible events can then begin to happen. You should always look for the small miracle around you in your life.

Angels are not a religious concept, but a spiritual one. Some religious institutions have embraced the concept of Angels a little more evidently, thus this association has developed. The appreciation of Angels, though, does not belong to only these institutions. Every person has Angels around them and every person has access to these Angels. A person can connect only with his or her own angels. They are around us constantly, waiting for us to ask for their help. When we seek their assistance, we might anticipate our request to be fulfilled with the precise and desired end result we want. It is a common expectation. The spiritual realm will, however, give us the assistance our situation needs, not the one we want. This is so, because the spiritual realm operates on the level of truth, for our highest good, not for our whims. To accept this truth from the spiritual realm, we must have trust.

To enable me to accomplish a Soul Healing for a person, they must initially have the belief and trust that this can happen. Nothing can happen to a person; it happens for a person. Prior to a healing, I have prepared my personal energy and the surrounding energy, by clearing and purifying it. My healing energy is a combination of various healing energies. When the person, with whom I am working, is initially relaxed, the clearing and welcoming of new energy into all the chakras of their spiritual body will happen. My hands become immediate sources of heat from the healing energy coming through me. I scan the person's energy field from about fifty centimeters above them, while they are lying down relaxed. Energy Healing has no need to make physical contact with the person, as the work is being done in the energy field. As I scan, I see the energy inside the body in colors and forms, which might reveal stuck energy, an issue with a vital organ or pain. The healing energy is directed to their energy to remove all plugs of energy. I then rescan to be shown the physical issues the person might be undergoing. Some pain can be alleviated instantly. Energy is also targeted at acupressure endpoints. Although there is no pressure with touch, the energy focuses a concentrated beam of light and energy, but the client would feel no discomfort. Energy impressing on these points achieves profound results, as it incorporates the entire energy network of the body. This procedure also dispels the energy remnants of conditions the person might have suffered within the past two weeks. Any supplementary residual body pain is more in-depth and can only be eradicated when the causal issue is dealt with. These issues might exist within the soul, or at the emotional or mental levels.

The Soul Healing then takes place. The term 'Soul Healing' is self-explanatory. When we have a complete and healed soul, our life is freed from all the internalized trauma, burdens and misery, which are obstructing our life. At the Soul healing, the essence, the center of the person representing the soul, is elevated to the highest vibrational levels of energy, to connect with their soul for the purpose of healing. Although I am now dealing with the soul, the image of the person I physically see is also the image the soul displays. I focus on guiding their soul to a peaceful place, which is a building of marble and palatial grandeur. This building is the most exquisite structure with tall, glassless windows radiating pure, white light. An open skylight allows white light to drift down and softly bathe the soul of the person. If this structure were on Earth, it would be a monument of the greatest magnificence and stateliness.

The person gently rises up to lie onto a section of what appears to be stone but is warm and soft to the touch. I begin the Soul Healing and am assisted by several guides. Initially, the Soul Reading is done, when I witness scenes from their early life, scenes from their present or scenes with people who have passed on and are in that room to support the person. I witness these scenes to bring this information to the person and help them identify those areas in their life, which need attention. Their soul is given the breath of healing from within that room, which is the most intense, white light I have ever seen. The soul now radiates as a brilliant white sphere, bathed in the glow of golden light. The soul is cleared of hurtful experiences, one by one. I am shown images of what transpired in the particular events. Less distressing events are dealt with collectively and healed together. If an event is more traumatic, then a separate healing will be focused on only that one event at a later occasion.

A very traumatic event would require that I find the missing soul energy part by viewing the explanatory image shown to me. The image would exhibit clues to me: the person at the age they were when the incident happened, the place it happened and other people who were involved. I would have to find the piece which presented all those aspects. This energy part is located within a band of high vibrational energy, where all the missing soul energy pieces exist. Guides assist in soul part retrieval, which is conducted at the highest and purest levels of vibrational energy. The piece is located and returned to the energy field at the front of the person so that they can welcome it during the Soul Healing. The complete procedure to reunite a soul part with the soul involves welcoming it during a Soul Healing and receiving and accepting it after the healing. Before the receiving can occur, a review of the traumatic event and the sensitive details this might raise would need to take place at the session. The client will be guided in the process of then receiving the soul part. The acceptance of the soul piece would happen privately for the client at their home. They will be given guidance in the acknowledgment of the traumatic incident. Acknowledgement does not imply that the person is expected to blame themselves or feel guilty; it is only an acknowledgement that the incident happened, the energy was created and that energy existed within their soul. Only by acknowledging its existence, are we then able to eliminate it. In their home, they can allow any residual emotions or thoughts to be released and then accept openly this soul part within their soul. Their soul is now more advanced with the inclusion of this piece.

During a Soul Healing, if I have received any 'secret' information pertaining to a traumatic event and have been given permission to disclose this to the person, I will share this information. I receive clear guidance on how to proceed. If no permission of disclosure was granted, I am still permitted to express the guidance in a manner to allow them to understand a particular incident, in order to help them reach a resolution.

During the healing, the client will have a visual and sensory experience. Some of the experiences people feel are flying, meeting people, being in a garden or being at a seashore. Each person's experience is unique and each healing is unique for the same person. No two healings are the same for me. A person will not be able to see what I see, although I can tap into what they are seeing and sensing.

Since I am able to speak with souls of the living as well as with the souls of those passed on, I might be given a message from the soul of a living person associated with the client. This person might have had difficulty in expressing themselves face to face with the client. The soul of this living person has chosen to be present in that session to take the opportunity to share required information through me, which poor communication had obstructed. I cannot demand a living soul to be present, as this would not be respecting their freewill. The client might also yearn to connect with a special departed person, but only those souls, who can bring the utmost benefit for the person, are present, which may or may not include the person they wish to contact. The souls present at a healing session are not determined by the client or myself, but by the spiritual realm.

At the completion of the healing, the soul of the client resumes its place at the elevated level and the essence returns to the spirit of the person. Usually, people will excitedly share stories with me of what they saw, what they felt and sensed. Some people will have viewed scenes unique to them. I describe to them what I witnessed and pass on all messages. It is, after all, their information, not mine and I pass it on in its entirety. I am the messenger, not the originator. These messages are profound for the client and clarity and healing will begin to happen.

If a vital organ is sick, I would have been told or shown this during the healing and I share this information with the client. They may be aware of this ailment and be receiving medical care, or this might be their first knowledge of it. This condition could be the manifestation of an underlying emotional or mental issue. If the issue is not of a traumatic nature, I can bring healing to the underlying issue that caused the ailing organ and this would remove the sickness and render the organ healthy. If the causal issue is more profound, this would necessitate a soul retrieval of the energy piece. The client would need to first acknowledge and confront the painful, underlying event, making this a more complicated process. Only after this was completed, would good health return to the vital organ.

When we use words in our daily life, they sometimes have a preconceived or ambiguous meaning for the listener. The words I am given in the messages transfer the untainted meaning and there is no need for interpretation. The source of this information only has our best interest. The messages are never general. They will contain a word or a name that is totally specific to the client. In this way, this information can readily be validated by the client. When I deliver these words to the client, I am speaking, but the words are coming from my soul. Even while sharing these messages with them, I might receive a further message. I might disregard it temporarily as I am speaking. The message is never lost and is usually persistent to be passed on, so the energy waits until I can receive it.

People, experiencing a Soul Healing, will ask how long the process lasted. The actual Soul Healing usually takes up to thirty minutes, but they may have felt as if it were five minutes, even though it took a great deal of time to describe their experiences. The mechanism of time is very different on the physical and spiritual levels. In fact, there is no such system as time on the spiritual level. When I take my journeys, I can recount the events, which lasted an hour, when I know I underwent the journey for only ten physical minutes. This is also true during hypnagogia, where one hour of activity during sleep can be experienced in three physical minutes. The brain waves and energy have a different concentration during wakefulness or hypnagogic sleep, producing the different perceptions of time.

The entire Soul Healing experience is very peaceful, gentle and perfect. There can be no other outcome at these highest pure energy levels. Over the past six years of Soul Healings, the results have been impressive. Each healing experience of a person has been distinct for me. I am given the most meaningful words, which resonate precisely with the client. I am always pleasantly surprised at how most of the information is validated by the person. Their reaction spans the emotions of tears to laughter. Issues are resolved, stress is released and lives are improved.

Following a discussion about the client's healing experience, they will clearly see what needs to be addressed or resolved in their life. Since these issues are usually numerous at the initial consult, I typically assign up to three tasks for the person to do before the next consult one month later. These tasks might involve reaching out to speak to a person they have ostracized, or understanding a childhood incident or rearranging an area where they meditate. Only their diligence in completing any tasks will bring them the reward of an improved life. When a client follows the suggested schedule of six healings spanning seven months, the final two healing consults will involve a Dynamic Soul Healing. This will access information at a profoundly deep level, which will only be possible to undertake when the person is at that stage after four prior healings. Generally, the six healings will produce a spiritual healing and ultimately, soul empowerment. It will lead to a complete understanding of the innermost depths of their being that they never knew they had, culminating in a complete soul.

It has been acknowledged that the symbolic veil, which figuratively separates the spiritual realm or universe from the physical realm, has progressively become thinner. This has happened from the increased intuition of a greater number of people to connect through it, to understand it. It is easier now to access the spiritual realm. This does not mean that it is easy to access the spiritual realm, but it is easier. Lifting this veil aside is not the impossible task it once was. I welcome and support some clients to take advantage of this. When the more spiritually aware clients, with whom I have worked for a few months, request and are given the tools to access the spiritual realm for themselves, they are pleasantly surprised at their prompt triumphs to empower their life. It involves a daily commitment to begin the day by spending ten minutes surrounding yourself and your family members with protective white light, to be grateful for having that day and to request well-defined help with certain tasks. Some of these tools would be used throughout the day, while the others are for the initial protection. In the entire waking day, the effort is comparatively minimal, but the rewards are vast.

If we are able to access the spiritual realm and further access our soul, we must examine why we are therefore so disconnected from our soul, especially as this separation seems to cause us so much hardship. There are very many people, who are not even aware of the possibility to access the soul. This ignorance does not appear very fair or just. The secrets of our lives are enveloped within the soul and many people are not even aware of the existence of the soul. My view is that it is anticipated that we would look to a higher power, at which time this soul connection would open up to us. This is much the same as a parent answering the questions from a child; the child has no knowledge of a particular fact until he asks and is given the answer. He now has that information. Similarly, we are looked after in this way, yet most of us cannot hear this guidance. Until a person is able to access the spiritual realm for themselves, I am the conduit for this, but I encourage them to acquire this ability. Throughout my own journey of soul discovery, I have merely asked if there is information I should know to help me lead a happier and more fulfilled life. I am always given the answers.

In asking questions, I learned that we should be grateful for the people and positive happenings in our life and say "thank you" many times a day. This is part of a cycle; we request a favorable event, which is granted and we say "thank you", enabling that cycle to complete and allowing the next cycle to begin. "Thank you" carries the same powerful energy in every language. It is the sentiment of "thank you", not the actual words.

When I bring the information to a person, it has immense significance, but how they receive it, will determine what value it will assume in their energy field and thus their life. When healers receive their accreditations, they take an oath to respect the ancient information shared with them and to ensure the guidance and information are honored in a way appropriate for that society. I deliver information, so, by virtue, it is not an item. Due to the nature of information as non-tangible, I have to ensure that my time is respected and not allow people to foster the belief that they are not receiving a tangible item and so do not need to honor it. The universe sees this in a very definite way; if the information is not honored, it will manifest the value placed on it by the end receiver.

Time is a commodity in our society. We have limited free time, which makes it valuable, thus it must be respected. The person has made the effort to travel and be present at my practice for one and a quarter hours. I will have already read their energy and collected messages for them for at least two hours prior to their arrival and will write up the events of the session for up to an hour after they leave. Each one-hour consult comprises four hours of my time and work. Since the guidance has to be honored, I ask only for one hour of compensation. This is my act of benevolence for humankind. Although some people might tell me that this is perhaps not the most rational use of my time, I am motivated by witnessing the tremendous results of improved lives for many people.

I am eternally grateful for the help that I receive from the spiritual realm. I am graciously given the information to pass on. It is always accurate. The person, who is receiving it, recognizes the value and benefits from it. The healing energy is so perfect that a person, open to receive it, will embrace it and see instantaneously the incredible results in their life.

11
ReBirth of the soul

The crux of this chapter can be summarized in the next sentence. The word 'hole' is contained in the word 'whole'. To re-include the letter 'w' into the word 'hole' represents a lengthy process and a great deal of dedication. Our goal is to complete the soul and become whole.

Empowering a life with healing energy of the highest vibrational levels will transform a person. Clearing our soul, healing our soul, evolving our soul will prompt a notable change in our life. A person can never again be the person they were. They will become an elevated and better version of that original person, empowered from the experience of the rebirth of their soul. We must first accede that we exist at all. A greater power has decided that our soul will exist and we came into being. Once in existence, we will endure eternally through our soul. Presently, our existence is confined to the earthly realm. When our body dies, we will cease the earthly existence and commence one in heaven. Our soul does not die. Only in an extreme circumstance, will the soul cease to exist. I have learned from the spiritual realm that a soul, which is responsible for horrific mass atrocities in the world, will be destroyed only after all instruction to help the soul have failed. This is the only time that the freewill of a soul will not be honored.

I am happy to appreciate that I, my soul, exist. It is difficult for my brain to understand profoundly that I am here. It is challenging to imagine what I would feel if I did not exist. Would I feel a void or feel anything at all? This concept of nothingness is more difficult to understand than one would anticipate. When I observe people, I appreciate that their souls were also chosen and created to exist. They are going about their daily lives oblivious to this. They believe that it is only their physical body, not their soul, which they require to maintain in a healthy condition. Their soul continues to exist without their knowledge. Their soul is transformed by the challenges in their life without their awareness. Their soul requires their attention to heal, but they are uninformed and unenlightened about this need. Thus their soul remains unevolved with the lessons of their trials becoming internalized as unwelcome energy in their body.

The soul holds the lessons, the positive emotions, the solutions to perplexities in our life and the missing energy created from trauma. It is an encapsulation of our life. It is a source of advance warning in a negative situation if we would only know to heed it; it gives us clarity in a situation; it has the resources to assist us to make the best choices. It is, in fact, yourself guiding yourself from a higher perception.

The uniqueness of each soul can be expressed as an analogy of music. Musical theory is very mathematical. It has a fundamental structure. Each note played is based on the mathematical system of scales and chords. When associated notes are put together, however, they harmonize and produce pleasant sounds, creating a piece of music. The same piece played by a variety of musicians will each have a distinct sound, as the musician has instilled into the notes their own expression, interpreting it with their emotions and their love of music. This is also true of the soul. It has a fundamental structure but is unique to only one person. We instill into it the subtleties of our encounters in life, our victories over challenges and our love. It echoes our personality, hence we have our basic personality intact when we reach heaven. We imprint our love and happiness onto it, which it will carry forever. With each encounter of love, the soul will shield it eternally and always make it available for the soul's person to draw upon.

It is essential that people live and enjoy today and not be perpetually looking to the future. If a special trip or event is planned for the end of the month, a person should not go through their days waiting for that day to arrive. Full respect must be given to the gift of those in-between days and to make them count, by doing something special during that time, such as talking with your family or going for a walk in the sunshine. That time will never be returned to you, so it should be respected and valued today. It is a gift from God. We need to find the balance in our life and live our life with that balance. The equilibrium in our life and our evolvement is perfection. We have merely to embrace this and bring it into our daily life.

We have a regiment of basic matters to which we must attend in our life: eat, wash, dress, earn money and pay for items and services. There is no choice in these activities and they take up a portion of our time. We must, therefore, be selective about what we choose to do for the remainder of our available time.

Without a doubt, life and our existence would be so much easier if we did not have to eat. There would not be the need for grocery stores, no food agriculture, no need to earn the money to buy the food, no restaurants including fast food establishments and no need to go food shopping or to spend the time preparing the food. There would also be no starvation, no obesity, no health issues from poor diet, no food poisoning and no immense healthcare costs to look after dietary issues, eating disorders or type 2 diabetes. Substantial resources of time and money would be immediately liberated. All these changes would result from the simple act of not having to eat. We question, therefore, why we are expected to undertake these routines. These practices do make us rely on each other and work together to achieve them. This leaves out of the balance, however, the people unable to earn money to buy the food. Their souls are just as valuable, but they have predetermined this situation before the commencement of their life in order to evolve through it. The manner in which this situation has turned into reality is perhaps now not so appealing to them. From this situation, however, grows the need for a group of volunteers to create a building to provide free food, cooked or conserved, for these people. The hunger of one group has evolved the souls of the caretaker group. Whether they are aware of this interconnection or not, their souls are linked and all souls have evolved.

We need to consistently empower our life so that we can generate the situations to advance our own soul or the soul of another. The only way this can be accomplished is by having awareness of our own soul. Many of us have gifts and abilities, which enable us to bring healing to others or to guide them to become aware of their spiritual level. We need to view these capabilities as an opportunity to bring more healing to all parts of the world. The world needs so much healing, that there is an immense amount of work for all of us.

Sadly, our world is in a mess. Events beyond our control are happening: hurricanes, wildfires, flooding, mudslides and frigid winter temperatures. Events of human fabrication are also happening: war, violence, family abuse and terrorism. Some people might say that all the aforementioned events are the creation of the human race. Compounded with this, there has been an escalation of mental health disorders, including PTSD, OCD, ADD, ADHD and AUD. These acronyms have become familiar to us and are the unfortunate representation of our society. Our world is in great turmoil. People absorb this unstable energy and live their lives, reflecting its failures and distortions.

This chaotic muddle solidly walls in our truth and our essence, so that they cannot be easily reached within us. We need to dismantle that wall of disorders by accessing our essence and connecting to our soul through the higher vibrational levels of energy. Reaching our source, we can cleanse it, clear it, regenerate it and direct it to assist us in both disassembling the wall and initiating our recovery beyond that point.

In order to activate your ability to help yourself, I encourage you to use *Soul Oneness Power©*. At this highest and purest level, the energy from God, all personal energy can be adjusted, resulting in the empowering of your life. An element of your life will change; an emotional hurt will be removed; baggage carried throughout your life, can finally be released; trauma abuse can be conclusively reconciled and eliminated; pain from the loss of a child can be unburdened. We have lived these events and we have endured them. Now is the time to bring healing to the pain. The lessons, now freed from the pain and shown in the light of understanding, can remain with us. The soul will become, once again, complete. The result of this will be the rebirth of the soul. The soul will have the resilience to encounter new challenges without undue suffering. The rebirth of the soul can be accomplished at any stage of a person's life, but, as soon as it is achieved, a person can begin to live a fulfilled and happy life. Now is the time for the soul.

My position is to bring healing to people. I am not naïve to believe this ability to bring healing is totally from my own self. I have always accepted that it emanates from a higher power. For me, this is God. Some people might believe that I have an ulterior motive to bring healing into their lives, as I might be taking the opportunity to explain that it comes from God and to make them believers in the process. This is not so. Healing is a gift available to everyone. People do not have to choose between God or being with cancer. I willingly bring the healing to everyone, believer or not.

During my early years of learning about this vast topic, I found I would gain a better understanding of a particular section of learning only after completing it, rather than while learning it. Perhaps the person questioning me is God's instrument, asking me many questions so that I might ponder the answers, because soon, I would need that information for others. In this way, my work, my own self and my life advanced continually.

I have evolved because I have chosen to do this. When I am sitting in front of a person after a healing, I can present to them the messages to resolve their issues, but if there is no reciprocal framework within them to accept this, the information will go nowhere. They have to be willing to make the effort and do the work. They have already made two great steps: they acknowledged they lacked the help and guidance they needed, and they showed up at my practice to receive this help and guidance. All of us go through life, but many of us make minimal effort to understand it. If this approach were to be applied, for example, to a new job, the consequences might illustrate why it is necessary to make the effort to understand life. If you showed up at a new job and were given no explanation about the duties and received no training so you simply sat at a desk, waiting in ignorance, would this be the criteria for a successful job? Would the employer or other employees notice your achievements? We cannot advance by making little or no effort while expecting awesome results. So it is in our entire life. If the benefits of healing are worth having in your life, they are worth working for.

Ultimately it is about the rebirth of our soul while we are living our earthly life. This is a dual purpose of life: to live the experiences of life and also to undertake the rebirth of the soul. Although we are on the Earth to find happiness and enjoyment, we are also here to learn and evolve. Much as we, as parents or teachers, guide children to be the best they can be in their life, so we too must learn our lessons and become the best person we can be.

This can best be illustrated by a real journey of a client. I will call her Jen. I met Jen when she attended one of my presentations and signed up for a healing consult. At the healing session, she was open-minded and very knowledgeable spiritually, so it was a pleasure to work with her. She had done a lot of spiritual work on herself but was unable to call herself 'whole', which was her intended goal. In each session, a major incident, which had caused her trauma, was uncovered. The emotional pain was released. The energy piece of the soul relating to that incident was retrieved and welcomed by me, then welcomed, received and accepted by Jen. She was surprised that those issues still influenced her life detrimentally, as she believed they had been dealt with. During her own work, she had handled the issue on a physical, emotional and spiritual level, but had not targeted and removed the residual energy, which was still contained within the soul. It still needed to be dealt with at the soul level. We addressed the unwelcome events in daily life, which would potentially occur as a result of this residual, damaging energy. Jen affirmed that this was in fact happening, by giving an example of a colleague addressing her in a very condescending manner. Jen believed that such an incident should not have happened as she was spiritually changed. She was changed, but she was not whole.

Jen's behavior during her formative years was fundamentally modified by traumatic incidents and affected her confidence, self-esteem and desire to be happy. She had sown seeds of doubt into her life, that she could ever be happy with a loving family, fulfilling career and her love of travelling. She felt undeserving of happiness. She had gone through the motions of marriage, children and a career. Each of these facets of her life was tarnished with her husband's illness, an estranged daughter and bullying by her co-workers.

During the sessions, messages from both living and departed people were shared and Jen validated them all. She came to know about the relatives who had passed on, whom she never got to know in her life. She learned that they were at her side to help her. She was not alone in her quest to become whole.

The fifth and penultimate session brought a huge shock. The Dynamic Soul Healing displayed to me a scene involving very inappropriate behavior to Jen. After the healing, I found myself with a dilemma. My brain had interceded and was questioning how such a brutal incident did not come up in one of the earlier sessions, so my brain concluded that it must be untrue. I quickly brought white light to myself, allowing my soul to take over. I had received this information and so was obliged to pass it on. As compassionately as I could, I described what I had witnessed and asked Jen if this had happened. She uttered only one word, "Yes". This would have overwhelmed me, had I not been handling this from my soul. I had returned with the soul energy piece relating to this incident and this was received by Jen. I counselled her about how to accept it at home. She would have to review this incident, but as an observer and not as a victim. This was successful. With the release of the energy of this horrifying incident, Jen's confidence increased and the affirmative results were immediate. She shared examples of people's more favorable responses to her when she exhibited confidence.

After the sixth and final session, Jen had clarity about the unproductive energy she had been carrying all her life. I showed her a meditation to unlink her consciousness from the past. This was a visualization of herself on a beach with sand and sea. She drew a line in the sand in front of her and stepped over in front of the line and stood there. The healing water from the sea ebbed in, touched her feet and then flowed back towards the sea taking away the unwanted energy. It was a 'goodbye' to the past. Once this residual energy had been removed and all the soul energy pieces had been accepted, she had achieved a complete soul. This enabled a rebirth of her soul, making her whole.

Her energy came into balance, thus her life came into balance. Jen's efforts from her own spiritual work and my involvement of nine months brought her the great results for which she had searched. It is probably not a coincidence that the rebirth of her soul spanned nine months, the period of gestation of a human being. Jen applied the diligence and hard work, relentlessly pushing forward through all the painful incidents she had to re-examine. The energy she radiated attracted positive energy from people and circumstances. Today, she has seen her husband's health improve, has re-established communication with her daughter and has a new job which showcases her many organizational talents, earning her respect and appreciation from her colleagues. She is happy, living a fulfilled life and is planning her next travel adventure.

It is important for us to nourish and keep our soul vital, even if we choose not to take a journey of soul rebirth, although this is the preferred course. The tool to connect with higher levels of vibrational energy to access the soul is available to everyone. Many people have their own method to make this connection. Accessing the library of helpful information within our soul of past trauma, present health issues and challenging circumstances will bring resolutions and avert future health issues and hazards in life. We should strive to be the best person we can be in our life.

We should determine what our life goals are. People usually have a goal of plentiful money. We observe that many prominent people have plenty of money, so we might conclude that having a lot of money equates to greatness. There could certainly be a very great woman or man, having wisdom, patience and service to others, but because they are unknown and financially poor, they might not be considered as great. Many people are unsung heroes, toiling for the good of others, so it is gratifying when a stranger might nominate them for recognition of greatness.

We each have greatness within ourselves; we need only to discover it. This will take time, which some people cannot spare as they are completely overwhelmed with the time-consuming routines of their day. If we did not have jobs, family commitments or errands, what would we do all day? Would we simply involve ourselves in pleasant pastimes and feel happy? We have our daily duties so that we might meet challenges and overcome them, thereby progressing in our knowledge and soul evolvement. Living our life is our work, not our pastime. This does not, however, preclude having a pastime in our life.

We all share the common physical and personal evolution from infant, to adult with immense potential and finally to become elderly. We all do not, however, share the common personal evolution of our soul. The physical development happens and is not a choice. The soul advancement will only happen by our choice. Even though we might not have the knowledge to begin, much less to accomplish this soul evolution, we can be assured that help is available to us. We need only request the help. We might already have an inkling that help does exist beyond the earthly realm. In the past, we have asked for assistance and an event happened, fulfilling our request. We might have tended to reason this away as a coincidence and ponder that perhaps it would have happened that way anyway. We will never know which way it would otherwise have happened, but rest assured that there are no coincidences.

In addition to receiving help from the spiritual realm, it is also available from God, or the other names by which people refer to Him, Omnipotence, All-Knowing, Source of Energy. Where does God feature in all of this living and evolving? He exists at that place beyond the capacity of our brain, where we can ask the questions and receive the answers. Here, we can be directed to our soul to receive the lessons. Here is where we know that we are unique, exceptional and that we are loved.

God can override any event we had predetermined for our life. We will be given knowledge, usually in a dream, if this is to happen. We too can initiate an override. We can request a change to or a cancellation of a predetermined event which has become a reality, but it is God's will whether this is actioned. Our lot is to accept His decision. I had a personal experience of this during my brother's illness. In a dream, I pleaded with God to grant my brother the miracle of getting through cancer and continuing to live. I was under the misconception that every person experiencing an illness wanted to live. With kindness, it was made very evident to me that my brother's wish to move on to the next phase of his soul's evolvement would be respected and that my desire to change this was futile. His decision was not changed. I had to embrace this into my soul and was reconciled to acceptance.

The journey of your soul is to have experiences presented to you, some of your choosing and some not of your volition. While undergoing the events of your younger life, the soul is incomplete. Facing the challenges of your adult life leaves imprints on the incomplete soul or causes energy pieces to become missing due to traumatic events. Addressing all the energy pieces, which were released as a result of trauma, brings about a regeneration of soul energy. When all the energy pieces have been retrieved, welcomed, received and accepted, the soul is now complete. It is this renewal which now supports the rebirth of your soul. The rebirth, enabled by your awareness of your soul, must first conclude for the soul and spirit to become whole. Once accomplished, a person is now whole. Being whole is sanctioned by incorporating the soul's knowledge into your life and living with the lessons. Life events will still continue to be experienced, but being in control of your life, your management of them will produce more positive results and avoid the reverberation of destructive effects throughout other elements of your life.

Complete. Rebirth. Whole. You finally found the 'W'!

Respect today. Make every today your best day. Look at the miracles around you. You are to live today like you have no tomorrows. Live with no regrets. Now is the time for you, valued reader, to heal and complete your soul, experience the rebirth of your soul and become whole. Your life will transform into a life with the potential for health, happiness and fulfillment.

Now is the time for your soul.

Notes

*When, where and how
I met my Soul*

www.ingramcontent.com/pod-product-compliance
Lightning Source LLC
Chambersburg PA
CBHW070633100426
42744CB00006B/663